Business Cost Optimization
Complete Self-Assessment Guide

The guidance in this Self-Assessment is based on Business Cost Optimization best practices and standards in business process architecture, design and quality management. The guidance is also based on the professional judgment of the individual collaborators listed in the Acknowledgments.

Table of Contents

About The Art of Service   8
Acknowledgments   9
Included Resources - how to access   10

Your feedback is invaluable to us   12
Purpose of this Self-Assessment   12
How to use the Self-Assessment   13
Business Cost Optimization
Scorecard Example   15

Business Cost Optimization
Scorecard   16

BEGINNING OF THE
SELF-ASSESSMENT: 17
CRITERION #1: RECOGNIZE   18

CRITERION #2: DEFINE: 30

CRITERION #3: MEASURE: 47

CRITERION #4: ANALYZE: 62

CRITERION #5: IMPROVE: 78

CRITERION #6: CONTROL: 95

CRITERION #7: SUSTAIN: 107
Business Cost Optimization and Managing Projects, Criteria
for Project Managers: 133
1.0 Initiating Process Group: Business Cost Optimization 134

1.1 Project Charter: Business Cost Optimization 136

1.2 Stakeholder Register: Business Cost Optimization 138

1.3 Stakeholder Analysis Matrix: Business Cost Optimization
139

2.0 Planning Process Group: Business Cost Optimization 141

2.1 Project Management Plan: Business Cost Optimization
143

2.2 Scope Management Plan: Business Cost Optimization
145

2.3 Requirements Management Plan: Business Cost
Optimization   147

2.4 Requirements Documentation: Business Cost
Optimization   149

2.5 Requirements Traceability Matrix: Business Cost
Optimization   151

2.6 Project Scope Statement: Business Cost Optimization 153

2.7 Assumption and Constraint Log: Business Cost
Optimization   156

2.8 Work Breakdown Structure: Business Cost Optimization
158

2.9 WBS Dictionary: Business Cost Optimization   160

2.10 Schedule Management Plan: Business Cost
Optimization   163

2.11 Activity List: Business Cost Optimization   165

2.12 Activity Attributes: Business Cost Optimization   167

2.13 Milestone List: Business Cost Optimization   169

2.14 Network Diagram: Business Cost Optimization   171

2.15 Activity Resource Requirements: Business Cost
Optimization   173

2.16 Resource Breakdown Structure: Business Cost
Optimization   174

2.17 Activity Duration Estimates: Business Cost Optimization
                                                       176

2.18 Duration Estimating Worksheet: Business Cost
Optimization   178

2.19 Project Schedule: Business Cost Optimization   180

2.20 Cost Management Plan: Business Cost Optimization 182

2.21 Activity Cost Estimates: Business Cost Optimization 184

2.22 Cost Estimating Worksheet: Business Cost Optimization
                                                       186

2.23 Cost Baseline: Business Cost Optimization   188

2.24 Quality Management Plan: Business Cost Optimization
                                                       190

2.25 Quality Metrics: Business Cost Optimization   192

2.26 Process Improvement Plan: Business Cost Optimization
                                                       194

2.27 Responsibility Assignment Matrix: Business Cost
Optimization   196

2.28 Roles and Responsibilities: Business Cost Optimization
                                                       198

2.29 Human Resource Management Plan: Business Cost Optimization 200

2.30 Communications Management Plan: Business Cost Optimization 202

2.31 Risk Management Plan: Business Cost Optimization 204

2.32 Risk Register: Business Cost Optimization 206

2.33 Probability and Impact Assessment: Business Cost Optimization 208

2.34 Probability and Impact Matrix: Business Cost Optimization 210

2.35 Risk Data Sheet: Business Cost Optimization 212

2.36 Procurement Management Plan: Business Cost Optimization 214

2.37 Source Selection Criteria: Business Cost Optimization 216

2.38 Stakeholder Management Plan: Business Cost Optimization 218

2.39 Change Management Plan: Business Cost Optimization 220

3.0 Executing Process Group: Business Cost Optimization 222

3.1 Team Member Status Report: Business Cost Optimization 224

3.2 Change Request: Business Cost Optimization 226

3.3 Change Log: Business Cost Optimization 228

3.4 Decision Log: Business Cost Optimization   230

3.5 Quality Audit: Business Cost Optimization   232

3.6 Team Directory: Business Cost Optimization   235

3.7 Team Operating Agreement: Business Cost Optimization
                                                             237

3.8 Team Performance Assessment: Business Cost
Optimization   239

3.9 Team Member Performance Assessment: Business Cost
Optimization   241

3.10 Issue Log: Business Cost Optimization   243

4.0 Monitoring and Controlling Process Group: Business Cost
Optimization   245

4.1 Project Performance Report: Business Cost Optimization
                                                             247

4.2 Variance Analysis: Business Cost Optimization   249

4.3 Earned Value Status: Business Cost Optimization   251

4.4 Risk Audit: Business Cost Optimization   253

4.5 Contractor Status Report: Business Cost Optimization 255

4.6 Formal Acceptance: Business Cost Optimization   257

5.0 Closing Process Group: Business Cost Optimization   259

5.1 Procurement Audit: Business Cost Optimization   261

5.2 Contract Close-Out: Business Cost Optimization   263

5.3 Project or Phase Close-Out: Business Cost Optimization
265

5.4 Lessons Learned: Business Cost Optimization   267
Index   269

About The Art of Service

The Art of Service, Business Process Architects since 2000, is dedicated to helping stakeholders achieve excellence.

Defining, designing, creating, and implementing a process to solve a stakeholders challenge or meet an objective is the most valuable role… In EVERY group, company, organization and department.

Unless you're talking a one-time, single-use project, there should be a process. Whether that process is managed and implemented by humans, AI, or a combination of the two, it needs to be designed by someone with a complex enough perspective to ask the right questions.

Someone capable of asking the right questions and step back and say, 'What are we really trying to accomplish here? And is there a different way to look at it?'

With The Art of Service's Standard Requirements Self-Assessments, we empower people who can do just that — whether their title is marketer, entrepreneur, manager, salesperson, consultant, Business Process Manager, executive assistant, IT Manager, CIO etc... —they are the people who rule the future. They are people who watch the process as it happens, and ask the right questions to make the process work better.

Contact us when you need any support with this Self-Assessment and any help with templates, blue-prints and examples of standard documents you might need:

http://theartofservice.com
service@theartofservice.com

Acknowledgments

This checklist was developed under the auspices of The Art of Service, chaired by Gerardus Blokdyk.

Representatives from several client companies participated in the preparation of this Self-Assessment.

In addition, we are thankful for the design and printing services provided.

Included Resources - how to access

Included with your purchase of the book is the Business Cost Optimization Self-Assessment Spreadsheet Dashboard which contains all questions and Self-Assessment areas and auto-generates insights, graphs, and project RACI planning - all with examples to get you started right away.

How? Simply send an email to
access@theartofservice.com
with this books' title in the subject to get the Business Cost Optimization Self Assessment Tool right away.

You will receive the following contents with New and Updated specific criteria:

- The latest quick edition of the book in PDF

- The latest complete edition of the book in PDF, which criteria correspond to the criteria in...

- The Self-Assessment Excel Dashboard, and...

- Example pre-filled Self-Assessment Excel Dashboard to get familiar with results generation

- In-depth specific Checklists covering the topic

- Project management checklists and templates to assist with implementation

INCLUDES LIFETIME SELF ASSESSMENT UPDATES

Every self assessment comes with Lifetime Updates and Lifetime Free Updated Books. Lifetime Updates is an industry-first feature which allows you to receive verified self assessment updates, ensuring you always have the most accurate information at your fingertips.

Get it now- you will be glad you did - do it now, before you forget.

Send an email to **access@theartofservice.com** with this books' title in the subject to get the Business Cost Optimization Self Assessment Tool right away.

Your feedback is invaluable to us

If you recently bought this book, we would love to hear from you! You can do this by writing a review on amazon (or the online store where you purchased this book) about your last purchase! As part of our continual service improvement process, we love to hear real client experiences and feedback.

How does it work?
To post a review on Amazon, just log in to your account and click on the Create Your Own Review button (under Customer Reviews) of the relevant product page. You can find examples of product reviews in Amazon. If you purchased from another online store, simply follow their procedures.

What happens when I submit my review?
Once you have submitted your review, send us an email at review@theartofservice.com with the link to your review so we can properly thank you for your feedback.

Purpose of this Self-Assessment

This Self-Assessment has been developed to improve understanding of the requirements and elements of Business Cost Optimization, based on best practices and standards in business process architecture, design and quality management.

It is designed to allow for a rapid Self-Assessment to determine how closely existing management practices and procedures correspond to the elements of the Self-Assessment.

The criteria of requirements and elements of Business Cost Optimization have been rephrased in the format of a Self-Assessment questionnaire, with a seven-criterion scoring system, as explained in this document.

In this format, even with limited background knowledge of

Business Cost Optimization, a manager can quickly review existing operations to determine how they measure up to the standards. This in turn can serve as the starting point of a 'gap analysis' to identify management tools or system elements that might usefully be implemented in the organization to help improve overall performance.

How to use the Self-Assessment

On the following pages are a series of questions to identify to what extent your Business Cost Optimization initiative is complete in comparison to the requirements set in standards.

To facilitate answering the questions, there is a space in front of each question to enter a score on a scale of '1' to '5'.

1 Strongly Disagree

2 Disagree

3 Neutral

4 Agree

5 Strongly Agree

Read the question and rate it with the following in front of mind:

**'In my belief,
the answer to this question is clearly defined'.**

There are two ways in which you can choose to interpret this statement;
1. how aware are you that the answer to the question is clearly defined
2. for more in-depth analysis you can choose to gather

evidence and confirm the answer to the question. This obviously will take more time, most Self-Assessment users opt for the first way to interpret the question and dig deeper later on based on the outcome of the overall Self-Assessment.

A score of '1' would mean that the answer is not clear at all, where a '5' would mean the answer is crystal clear and defined. Leave emtpy when the question is not applicable or you don't want to answer it, you can skip it without affecting your score. Write your score in the space provided.

After you have responded to all the appropriate statements in each section, compute your average score for that section, using the formula provided, and round to the nearest tenth. Then transfer to the corresponding spoke in the Business Cost Optimization Scorecard on the second next page of the Self-Assessment.

Your completed Business Cost Optimization Scorecard will give you a clear presentation of which Business Cost Optimization areas need attention.

Business Cost Optimization Scorecard Example

Example of how the finalized Scorecard can look like:

Business Cost Optimization Scorecard

Your Scores:

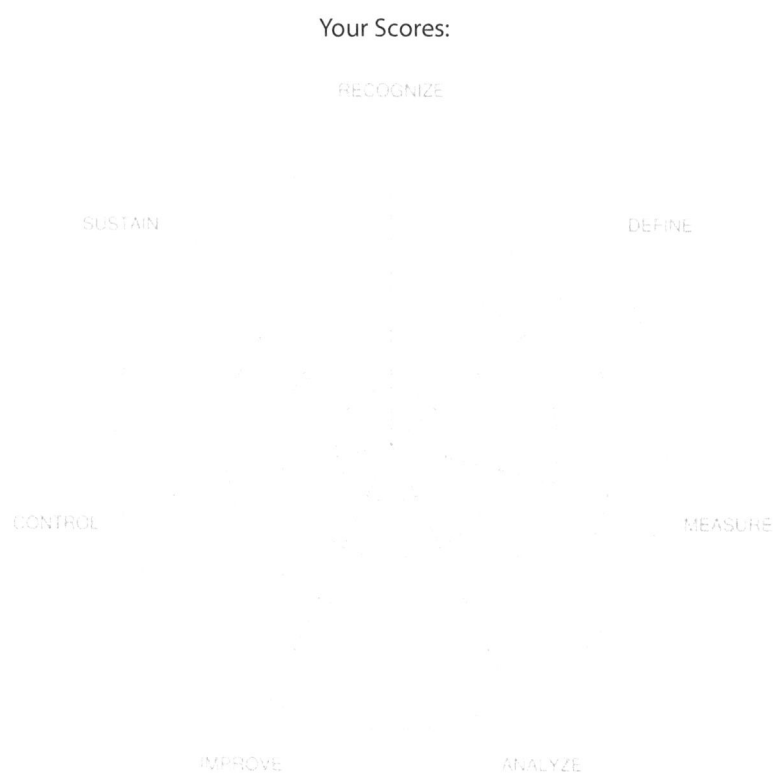

RECOGNIZE

SUSTAIN

DEFINE

CONTROL

MEASURE

IMPROVE

ANALYZE

BEGINNING OF THE SELF-ASSESSMENT:

CRITERION #1: RECOGNIZE

INTENT: Be aware of the need for change. Recognize that there is an unfavorable variation, problem or symptom.

In my belief, the answer to this question is clearly defined:

5 Strongly Agree

4 Agree

3 Neutral

2 Disagree

1 Strongly Disagree

1. Who needs budgets?
<--- Score

2. How does it fit into your organizational needs and tasks?
<--- Score

3. What is the smallest subset of the problem you can usefully solve?

<--- Score

4. What prevents you from making the changes you know will make you a more effective Business Cost Optimization leader?
<--- Score

5. How can auditing be a preventative security measure?
<--- Score

6. Which issues are too important to ignore?
<--- Score

7. Who needs to know about Business Cost Optimization?
<--- Score

8. What is the extent or complexity of the Business Cost Optimization problem?
<--- Score

9. Whom do you really need or want to serve?
<--- Score

10. What are the clients issues and concerns?
<--- Score

11. What is the problem or issue?
<--- Score

12. What are the Business Cost Optimization resources needed?
<--- Score

13. What do you need to start doing?

<--- Score

14. Are there recognized Business Cost Optimization problems?
<--- Score

15. Are there regulatory / compliance issues?
<--- Score

16. What training and capacity building actions are needed to implement proposed reforms?
<--- Score

17. When a Business Cost Optimization manager recognizes a problem, what options are available?
<--- Score

18. Will a response program recognize when a crisis occurs and provide some level of response?
<--- Score

19. How do you take a forward-looking perspective in identifying Business Cost Optimization research related to market response and models?
<--- Score

20. Which needs are not included or involved?
<--- Score

21. Would you recognize a threat from the inside?
<--- Score

22. What creative shifts do you need to take?
<--- Score

23. Do you have/need 24-hour access to key

personnel?
<--- Score

24. How many trainings, in total, are needed?
<--- Score

25. Consider your own Business Cost Optimization project, what types of organizational problems do you think might be causing or affecting your problem, based on the work done so far?
<--- Score

26. Who are your key stakeholders who need to sign off?
<--- Score

27. What is the recognized need?
<--- Score

28. To what extent would your organization benefit from being recognized as a award recipient?
<--- Score

29. Are there Business Cost Optimization problems defined?
<--- Score

30. Can management personnel recognize the monetary benefit of Business Cost Optimization?
<--- Score

31. What are the stakeholder objectives to be achieved with Business Cost Optimization?
<--- Score

32. Who else hopes to benefit from it?

<--- Score

33. Have you identified your Business Cost Optimization key performance indicators?
<--- Score

34. Think about the people you identified for your Business Cost Optimization project and the project responsibilities you would assign to them, what kind of training do you think they would need to perform these responsibilities effectively?
<--- Score

35. What Business Cost Optimization capabilities do you need?
<--- Score

36. What is the Business Cost Optimization problem definition? What do you need to resolve?
<--- Score

37. What Business Cost Optimization coordination do you need?
<--- Score

38. Do you recognize Business Cost Optimization achievements?
<--- Score

39. What information do users need?
<--- Score

40. Are losses recognized in a timely manner?
<--- Score

41. Why the need?

<--- Score

42. Are there any specific expectations or concerns about the Business Cost Optimization team, Business Cost Optimization itself?
<--- Score

43. What situation(s) led to this Business Cost Optimization Self Assessment?
<--- Score

44. Are there any revenue recognition issues?
<--- Score

45. What else needs to be measured?
<--- Score

46. How are you going to measure success?
<--- Score

47. How do you assess your Business Cost Optimization workforce capability and capacity needs, including skills, competencies, and staffing levels?
<--- Score

48. Where do you need to exercise leadership?
<--- Score

49. Who should resolve the Business Cost Optimization issues?
<--- Score

50. What are the timeframes required to resolve each of the issues/problems?
<--- Score

51. Will it solve real problems?

<--- Score

52. Is the quality assurance team identified?

<--- Score

53. As a sponsor, customer or management, how important is it to meet goals, objectives?

<--- Score

54. What needs to be done?

<--- Score

55. What are the minority interests and what amount of minority interests can be recognized?

<--- Score

56. Is it needed?

<--- Score

57. Looking at each person individually – does every one have the qualities which are needed to work in this group?

<--- Score

58. What would happen if Business Cost Optimization weren't done?

<--- Score

59. Do you need to avoid or amend any Business Cost Optimization activities?

<--- Score

60. How are the Business Cost Optimization's objectives aligned to the group's overall stakeholder

strategy?
<--- Score

61. What vendors make products that address the Business Cost Optimization needs?

<--- Score

62. Who needs to know?

<--- Score

63. What are the expected benefits of Business Cost Optimization to the stakeholder?
<--- Score

64. Are your goals realistic? Do you need to redefine your problem? Perhaps the problem has changed or maybe you have reached your goal and need to set a new one?
<--- Score

65. What resources or support might you need?
<--- Score

66. Does your organization need more Business Cost Optimization education?
<--- Score

67. Who defines the rules in relation to any given issue?
<--- Score

68. What activities does the governance board need to consider?
<--- Score

69. What are your needs in relation to Business

Cost Optimization skills, labor, equipment, and markets?
<--- Score

70. How do you recognize an objection?
<--- Score

71. Are employees recognized or rewarded for performance that demonstrates the highest levels of integrity?
<--- Score

72. Are controls defined to recognize and contain problems?
<--- Score

73. Does Business Cost Optimization create potential expectations in other areas that need to be recognized and considered?
<--- Score

74. Will Business Cost Optimization deliverables need to be tested and, if so, by whom?
<--- Score

75. Do you need different information or graphics?
<--- Score

76. How do you recognize an Business Cost Optimization objection?
<--- Score

77. How are training requirements identified?
<--- Score

78. What extra resources will you need?

<--- Score

79. What do employees need in the short term?
<--- Score

80. What should be considered when identifying available resources, constraints, and deadlines?
<--- Score

81. Why is this needed?
<--- Score

82. Where is training needed?
<--- Score

83. Is it clear when you think of the day ahead of you what activities and tasks you need to complete?
<--- Score

84. Are problem definition and motivation clearly presented?
<--- Score

85. What problems are you facing and how do you consider Business Cost Optimization will circumvent those obstacles?
<--- Score

86. How do you identify the kinds of information that you will need?
<--- Score

87. How much are sponsors, customers, partners, stakeholders involved in Business Cost Optimization? In other words, what are the risks, if Business Cost Optimization does not deliver successfully?

<--- Score

88. What Business Cost Optimization problem should be solved?

<--- Score

89. Do you know what you need to know about Business Cost Optimization?

<--- Score

90. Is the need for organizational change recognized?

<--- Score

91. What Business Cost Optimization events should you attend?

<--- Score

92. Which information does the Business Cost Optimization business case need to include?

<--- Score

93. What needs to stay?

<--- Score

94. What does Business Cost Optimization success mean to the stakeholders?

<--- Score

95. What is the problem and/or vulnerability?

<--- Score

96. What tools and technologies are needed for a custom Business Cost Optimization project?

<--- Score

97. Did you miss any major Business Cost

Optimization issues?
<--- Score

Add up total points for this section:
_ _ _ _ _ = Total points for this section

Divided by: _ _ _ _ _ _ (number of
statements answered) = _ _ _ _ _ _
Average score for this section

Transfer your score to the Business Cost
Optimization Index at the beginning of
the Self-Assessment.

CRITERION #2: DEFINE:

INTENT: Formulate the stakeholder problem. Define the problem, needs and objectives.

In my belief, the answer to this question is clearly defined:

5 Strongly Agree

4 Agree

3 Neutral

2 Disagree

1 Strongly Disagree

1. Is there a Business Cost Optimization management charter, including stakeholder case, problem and goal statements, scope, milestones, roles and responsibilities, communication plan?
<--- Score

2. Has a high-level 'as is' process map been completed, verified and validated?
<--- Score

3. Are task requirements clearly defined?
<--- Score

4. Has your scope been defined?
<--- Score

5. Do you all define Business Cost Optimization in the same way?
<--- Score

6. How do you manage scope?
<--- Score

7. Who are the Business Cost Optimization improvement team members, including Management Leads and Coaches?
<--- Score

8. What are the compelling stakeholder reasons for embarking on Business Cost Optimization?
<--- Score

9. How do you catch Business Cost Optimization definition inconsistencies?
<--- Score

10. What are the Business Cost Optimization use cases?
<--- Score

11. How would you define Business Cost Optimization leadership?
<--- Score

12. Are accountability and ownership for Business

Cost Optimization clearly defined?
<--- Score

13. When is the estimated completion date?
<--- Score

14. What system do you use for gathering Business Cost Optimization information?
<--- Score

15. Are the Business Cost Optimization requirements complete?
<--- Score

16. Has everyone on the team, including the team leaders, been properly trained?
<--- Score

17. What was the context?
<--- Score

18. How have you defined all Business Cost Optimization requirements first?
<--- Score

19. How do you manage unclear Business Cost Optimization requirements?
<--- Score

20. What are the tasks and definitions?
<--- Score

21. What information do you gather?
<--- Score

22. Has a Business Cost Optimization requirement not

been met?
<--- Score

23. What gets examined?
<--- Score

24. Is the Business Cost Optimization scope manageable?
<--- Score

25. Is data collected and displayed to better understand customer(s) critical needs and requirements.
<--- Score

26. Has the Business Cost Optimization work been fairly and/or equitably divided and delegated among team members who are qualified and capable to perform the work? Has everyone contributed?
<--- Score

27. How and when will the baselines be defined?
<--- Score

28. How would you define the culture at your organization, how susceptible is it to Business Cost Optimization changes?
<--- Score

29. Are approval levels defined for contracts and supplements to contracts?
<--- Score

30. How do you keep key subject matter experts in the loop?
<--- Score

31. Do you have organizational privacy requirements?
<--- Score

32. What would be the goal or target for a Business Cost Optimization's improvement team?
<--- Score

33. What are the dynamics of the communication plan?
<--- Score

34. What scope to assess?
<--- Score

35. Is the team adequately staffed with the desired cross-functionality? If not, what additional resources are available to the team?
<--- Score

36. Are the Business Cost Optimization requirements testable?
<--- Score

37. How can the value of Business Cost Optimization be defined?
<--- Score

38. Scope of sensitive information?
<--- Score

39. What are the Roles and Responsibilities for each team member and its leadership? Where is this documented?
<--- Score

40. What defines best in class?

<--- Score

41. How do you gather requirements?

<--- Score

42. Is Business Cost Optimization linked to key stakeholder goals and objectives?

<--- Score

43. Are there any constraints known that bear on the ability to perform Business Cost Optimization work? How is the team addressing them?

<--- Score

44. Is there any additional Business Cost Optimization definition of success?

<--- Score

45. Has/have the customer(s) been identified?

<--- Score

46. Is there regularly 100% attendance at the team meetings? If not, have appointed substitutes attended to preserve cross-functionality and full representation?

<--- Score

47. Are different versions of process maps needed to account for the different types of inputs?

<--- Score

48. Are roles and responsibilities formally defined?

<--- Score

49. What is a worst-case scenario for losses?

<--- Score

50. What are the boundaries of the scope? What is in bounds and what is not? What is the start point? What is the stop point?
<--- Score

51. Are required metrics defined, what are they?
<--- Score

52. Who defines (or who defined) the rules and roles?
<--- Score

53. Where can you gather more information?
<--- Score

54. Do you have a Business Cost Optimization success story or case study ready to tell and share?
<--- Score

55. How will variation in the actual durations of each activity be dealt with to ensure that the expected Business Cost Optimization results are met?
<--- Score

56. Is Business Cost Optimization currently on schedule according to the plan?
<--- Score

57. Is Business Cost Optimization required?
<--- Score

58. Is full participation by members in regularly held team meetings guaranteed?
<--- Score

59. Is the current 'as is' process being followed? If not, what are the discrepancies?

<--- Score

60. What key stakeholder process output measure(s) does Business Cost Optimization leverage and how?

<--- Score

61. Are customer(s) identified and segmented according to their different needs and requirements?

<--- Score

62. When are meeting minutes sent out? Who is on the distribution list?

<--- Score

63. What scope do you want your strategy to cover?

<--- Score

64. What happens if Business Cost Optimization's scope changes?

<--- Score

65. Do the problem and goal statements meet the SMART criteria (specific, measurable, attainable, relevant, and time-bound)?

<--- Score

66. How does the Business Cost Optimization manager ensure against scope creep?

<--- Score

67. What are the record-keeping requirements of Business Cost Optimization activities?

<--- Score

68. Have the customer needs been translated into specific, measurable requirements? How?
<--- Score

69. How do you manage changes in Business Cost Optimization requirements?
<--- Score

70. Does the team have regular meetings?
<--- Score

71. Who approved the Business Cost Optimization scope?
<--- Score

72. If substitutes have been appointed, have they been briefed on the Business Cost Optimization goals and received regular communications as to the progress to date?
<--- Score

73. Is there a clear Business Cost Optimization case definition?
<--- Score

74. Will a Business Cost Optimization production readiness review be required?
<--- Score

75. How is the team tracking and documenting its work?
<--- Score

76. When is/was the Business Cost Optimization start date?
<--- Score

77. What is the worst case scenario?
<--- Score

78. Have specific policy objectives been defined?
<--- Score

79. Are resources adequate for the scope?
<--- Score

80. Who is gathering information?
<--- Score

81. How do you hand over Business Cost Optimization context?
<--- Score

82. How was the 'as is' process map developed, reviewed, verified and validated?
<--- Score

83. Is scope creep really all bad news?
<--- Score

84. What is in the scope and what is not in scope?
<--- Score

85. What are the rough order estimates on cost savings/opportunities that Business Cost Optimization brings?
<--- Score

86. What are the core elements of the Business Cost Optimization business case?
<--- Score

87. Does the scope remain the same?
<--- Score

88. What is out of scope?
<--- Score

89. Is the scope of Business Cost Optimization defined?
<--- Score

90. Has the direction changed at all during the course of Business Cost Optimization? If so, when did it change and why?
<--- Score

91. What is the definition of Business Cost Optimization excellence?
<--- Score

92. Are all requirements met?
<--- Score

93. How do you gather Business Cost Optimization requirements?
<--- Score

94. The political context: who holds power?
<--- Score

95. Is the Business Cost Optimization scope complete and appropriately sized?
<--- Score

96. What is the definition of success?
<--- Score

97. Will team members regularly document their Business Cost Optimization work?

<--- Score

98. What Business Cost Optimization requirements should be gathered?

<--- Score

99. Has a project plan, Gantt chart, or similar been developed/completed?

<--- Score

100. What is the scope of Business Cost Optimization?

<--- Score

101. What is the scope of the Business Cost Optimization effort?

<--- Score

102. How will the Business Cost Optimization team and the group measure complete success of Business Cost Optimization?

<--- Score

103. Is special Business Cost Optimization user knowledge required?

<--- Score

104. What constraints exist that might impact the team?

<--- Score

105. How often are the team meetings?

<--- Score

106. Are there different segments of customers?
<--- Score

107. What is out-of-scope initially?
<--- Score

108. Has a team charter been developed and communicated?
<--- Score

109. Is the improvement team aware of the different versions of a process: what they think it is vs. what it actually is vs. what it should be vs. what it could be?
<--- Score

110. What information should you gather?
<--- Score

111. How are consistent Business Cost Optimization definitions important?
<--- Score

112. What is in scope?
<--- Score

113. What specifically is the problem? Where does it occur? When does it occur? What is its extent?
<--- Score

114. What critical content must be communicated – who, what, when, where, and how?
<--- Score

115. How do you build the right business case?
<--- Score

116. Have all of the relationships been defined properly?
<--- Score

117. What intelligence can you gather?
<--- Score

118. Will team members perform Business Cost Optimization work when assigned and in a timely fashion?
<--- Score

119. Has anyone else (internal or external to the group) attempted to solve this problem or a similar one before? If so, what knowledge can be leveraged from these previous efforts?
<--- Score

120. Is the team equipped with available and reliable resources?
<--- Score

121. Has the improvement team collected the 'voice of the customer' (obtained feedback – qualitative and quantitative)?
<--- Score

122. Are audit criteria, scope, frequency and methods defined?
<--- Score

123. How did the Business Cost Optimization manager receive input to the development of a Business Cost Optimization improvement plan and the estimated completion dates/times of each activity?
<--- Score

124. What sort of initial information to gather?
<--- Score

125. Is there a completed, verified, and validated high-level 'as is' (not 'should be' or 'could be') stakeholder process map?
<--- Score

126. How do you gather the stories?
<--- Score

127. Why are you doing Business Cost Optimization and what is the scope?
<--- Score

128. What are the Business Cost Optimization tasks and definitions?
<--- Score

129. Is it clearly defined in and to your organization what you do?
<--- Score

130. What sources do you use to gather information for a Business Cost Optimization study?
<--- Score

131. What are (control) requirements for Business Cost Optimization Information?
<--- Score

132. What customer feedback methods were used to solicit their input?
<--- Score

133. In what way can you redefine the criteria of choice clients have in your category in your favor?
<--- Score

134. Is there a completed SIPOC representation, describing the Suppliers, Inputs, Process, Outputs, and Customers?
<--- Score

135. What are the requirements for audit information?
<--- Score

136. How do you think the partners involved in Business Cost Optimization would have defined success?
<--- Score

137. What is the scope of the Business Cost Optimization work?
<--- Score

138. Is there a critical path to deliver Business Cost Optimization results?
<--- Score

Add up total points for this section:
_ _ _ _ _ = Total points for this section

Divided by: _ _ _ _ _ _ (number of statements answered) = _ _ _ _ _ _
Average score for this section

Transfer your score to the Business Cost Optimization Index at the beginning of

the Self-Assessment.

CRITERION #3: MEASURE:

In my belief, the answer to this
question is clearly defined:

5 Strongly Agree

4 Agree

3 Neutral

2 Disagree

1 Strongly Disagree

1. How do you verify the authenticity of the data and information used?
<--- Score

2. Is the cost worth the Business Cost Optimization effort ?
<--- Score

3. Are you taking your company in the direction of

better and revenue or cheaper and cost?
<--- Score

4. What could cause you to change course?
<--- Score

5. Where is the cost?
<--- Score

6. Has a cost center been established?
<--- Score

7. How is progress measured?
<--- Score

8. What causes mismanagement?
<--- Score

9. How can you reduce costs?
<--- Score

10. How are you verifying it?
<--- Score

11. How will you measure success?
<--- Score

12. What are your operating costs?
<--- Score

13. What causes extra work or rework?
<--- Score

14. How do your measurements capture actionable Business Cost Optimization information for use in exceeding your customers expectations and securing

your customers engagement?

<--- Score

15. How are measurements made?

<--- Score

16. When are costs are incurred?

<--- Score

17. How sensitive must the Business Cost Optimization strategy be to cost?

<--- Score

18. Are the units of measure consistent?

<--- Score

19. Are the Business Cost Optimization benefits worth its costs?

<--- Score

20. What measurements are possible, practicable and meaningful?

<--- Score

21. How can you measure the performance?

<--- Score

22. What are the costs of delaying Business Cost Optimization action?

<--- Score

23. What are the Business Cost Optimization investment costs?

<--- Score

24. What can be used to verify compliance?

<--- Score

25. What do you measure and why?
<--- Score

26. Have you included everything in your Business Cost Optimization cost models?
<--- Score

27. Does management have the right priorities among projects?
<--- Score

28. Who is involved in verifying compliance?
<--- Score

29. How do you prevent mis-estimating cost?
<--- Score

30. Are indirect costs charged to the Business Cost Optimization program?
<--- Score

31. Does the Business Cost Optimization task fit the client's priorities?
<--- Score

32. How do you measure lifecycle phases?
<--- Score

33. What are the Business Cost Optimization key cost drivers?
<--- Score

34. How are costs allocated?
<--- Score

35. What relevant entities could be measured?
<--- Score

36. What are the costs and benefits?
<--- Score

37. How do you measure variability?
<--- Score

38. Who should receive measurement reports?
<--- Score

39. How is performance measured?
<--- Score

40. Have you made assumptions about the shape of the future, particularly its impact on your customers and competitors?
<--- Score

41. What are you verifying?
<--- Score

42. Where is it measured?
<--- Score

43. How much does it cost?
<--- Score

44. How do you quantify and qualify impacts?
<--- Score

45. How to cause the change?
<--- Score

46. What are the uncertainties surrounding estimates of impact?
<--- Score

47. What is the Business Cost Optimization business impact?
<--- Score

48. What are the types and number of measures to use?
<--- Score

49. Why a Business Cost Optimization focus?
<--- Score

50. What potential environmental factors impact the Business Cost Optimization effort?
<--- Score

51. How do you measure success?
<--- Score

52. What is your decision requirements diagram?
<--- Score

53. What could cause delays in the schedule?
<--- Score

54. Does a Business Cost Optimization quantification method exist?
<--- Score

55. What methods are feasible and acceptable to estimate the impact of reforms?
<--- Score

56. What does a Test Case verify?

<--- Score

57. What are the estimated costs of proposed changes?

<--- Score

58. Do the benefits outweigh the costs?

<--- Score

59. What does losing customers cost your organization?

<--- Score

60. What is measured? Why?

<--- Score

61. Are missed Business Cost Optimization opportunities costing your organization money?

<--- Score

62. How will costs be allocated?

<--- Score

63. How can you reduce the costs of obtaining inputs?

<--- Score

64. Is it possible to estimate the impact of unanticipated complexity such as wrong or failed assumptions, feedback, etcetera on proposed reforms?

<--- Score

65. What does verifying compliance entail?

<--- Score

66. What are your customers expectations and measures?
<--- Score

67. Do you aggressively reward and promote the people who have the biggest impact on creating excellent Business Cost Optimization services/ products?
<--- Score

68. Do you have an issue in getting priority?
<--- Score

69. Do you have any cost Business Cost Optimization limitation requirements?
<--- Score

70. What causes innovation to fail or succeed in your organization?
<--- Score

71. Do you effectively measure and reward individual and team performance?
<--- Score

72. Is the solution cost-effective?
<--- Score

73. What would be a real cause for concern?
<--- Score

74. How do you verify if Business Cost Optimization is built right?
<--- Score

75. What are allowable costs?
<--- Score

76. Why do you expend time and effort to implement measurement, for whom?
<--- Score

77. What evidence is there and what is measured?
<--- Score

78. What are your primary costs, revenues, assets?
<--- Score

79. Which measures and indicators matter?
<--- Score

80. What do people want to verify?
<--- Score

81. What is the root cause(s) of the problem?
<--- Score

82. How do you verify and develop ideas and innovations?
<--- Score

83. What is an unallowable cost?
<--- Score

84. Are there any easy-to-implement alternatives to Business Cost Optimization? Sometimes other solutions are available that do not require the cost implications of a full-blown project?
<--- Score

85. Are Business Cost Optimization vulnerabilities

categorized and prioritized?
<--- Score

86. How do you aggregate measures across priorities?
<--- Score

87. How frequently do you verify your Business Cost Optimization strategy?
<--- Score

88. What are your key Business Cost Optimization organizational performance measures, including key short and longer-term financial measures?
<--- Score

89. What causes investor action?
<--- Score

90. What is the total cost related to deploying Business Cost Optimization, including any consulting or professional services?
<--- Score

91. What is the cause of any Business Cost Optimization gaps?
<--- Score

92. What is your Business Cost Optimization quality cost segregation study?
<--- Score

93. What harm might be caused?
<--- Score

94. How will your organization measure success?
<--- Score

95. Where can you go to verify the info?

<--- Score

96. Why do the measurements/indicators matter?

<--- Score

97. What is the cost of rework?

<--- Score

98. What drives O&M cost?

<--- Score

99. What disadvantage does this cause for the user?

<--- Score

100. How do you verify performance?

<--- Score

101. How will you measure your Business Cost Optimization effectiveness?

<--- Score

102. What happens if cost savings do not materialize?

<--- Score

103. At what cost?

<--- Score

104. Do you verify that corrective actions were taken?

<--- Score

105. What users will be impacted?

<--- Score

106. What are hidden Business Cost Optimization quality costs?

<--- Score

107. How do you verify Business Cost Optimization completeness and accuracy?

<--- Score

108. Is there an opportunity to verify requirements?

<--- Score

109. When a disaster occurs, who gets priority?

<--- Score

110. How can a Business Cost Optimization test verify your ideas or assumptions?

<--- Score

111. How will measures be used to manage and adapt?

<--- Score

112. What are the costs of reform?

<--- Score

113. When should you bother with diagrams?

<--- Score

114. How do you verify your resources?

<--- Score

115. What are the operational costs after Business Cost Optimization deployment?

<--- Score

116. Which costs should be taken into account?

<--- Score

117. How do you control the overall costs of your work processes?

<--- Score

118. How do you measure efficient delivery of Business Cost Optimization services?

<--- Score

119. Have design-to-cost goals been established?

<--- Score

120. Are actual costs in line with budgeted costs?

<--- Score

121. What are the current costs of the Business Cost Optimization process?

<--- Score

122. Among the Business Cost Optimization product and service cost to be estimated, which is considered hardest to estimate?

<--- Score

123. How do you verify the Business Cost Optimization requirements quality?

<--- Score

124. How will effects be measured?

<--- Score

125. Are supply costs steady or fluctuating?

<--- Score

126. Are you able to realize any cost savings?
<--- Score

127. Who pays the cost?
<--- Score

128. What does your operating model cost?
<--- Score

129. How can you measure Business Cost Optimization in a systematic way?
<--- Score

130. What measurements are being captured?
<--- Score

131. What is the total fixed cost?
<--- Score

132. How do you verify and validate the Business Cost Optimization data?
<--- Score

133. How can you manage cost down?
<--- Score

134. Are there competing Business Cost Optimization priorities?
<--- Score

135. Did you tackle the cause or the symptom?
<--- Score

136. How is the value delivered by Business Cost Optimization being measured?

<--- Score

Add up total points for this section:
_ _ _ _ _ = Total points for this section

Divided by: _ _ _ _ _ _ (number of
statements answered) = _ _ _ _ _ _
Average score for this section

Transfer your score to the Business Cost
Optimization Index at the beginning of
the Self-Assessment.

CRITERION #4: ANALYZE:

INTENT: Analyze causes, assumptions
and hypotheses.

In my belief, the answer to this
question is clearly defined:

5 Strongly Agree

4 Agree

3 Neutral

2 Disagree

1 Strongly Disagree

1. How do your work systems and key work processes relate to and capitalize on your core competencies?
<--- Score

2. How has the Business Cost Optimization data been gathered?
<--- Score

3. What information qualified as important?

<--- Score

4. How do mission and objectives affect the Business Cost Optimization processes of your organization?
<--- Score

5. An organizationally feasible system request is one that considers the mission, goals and objectives of the organization, key questions are: is the Business Cost Optimization solution request practical and will it solve a problem or take advantage of an opportunity to achieve company goals?
<--- Score

6. Where can you get qualified talent today?
<--- Score

7. Who qualifies to gain access to data?
<--- Score

8. Are all staff in core Business Cost Optimization subjects Highly Qualified?
<--- Score

9. Is the Business Cost Optimization process severely broken such that a re-design is necessary?
<--- Score

10. Where is Business Cost Optimization data gathered?
<--- Score

11. Do your employees have the opportunity to do what they do best everyday?
<--- Score

12. Can you add value to the current Business Cost Optimization decision-making process (largely qualitative) by incorporating uncertainty modeling (more quantitative)?
<--- Score

13. Do your leaders quickly bounce back from setbacks?
<--- Score

14. What Business Cost Optimization data do you gather or use now?
<--- Score

15. Was a detailed process map created to amplify critical steps of the 'as is' stakeholder process?
<--- Score

16. How much data can be collected in the given timeframe?
<--- Score

17. Were Pareto charts (or similar) used to portray the 'heavy hitters' (or key sources of variation)?
<--- Score

18. What resources go in to get the desired output?
<--- Score

19. Is pre-qualification of suppliers carried out?
<--- Score

20. How is the Business Cost Optimization Value Stream Mapping managed?
<--- Score

21. Is there a strict change management process?
<--- Score

22. Do staff qualifications match your project?
<--- Score

23. Think about some of the processes you undertake within your organization, which do you own?
<--- Score

24. Record-keeping requirements flow from the records needed as inputs, outputs, controls and for transformation of a Business Cost Optimization process, are the records needed as inputs to the Business Cost Optimization process available?
<--- Score

25. How was the detailed process map generated, verified, and validated?
<--- Score

26. Are all team members qualified for all tasks?
<--- Score

27. How will the change process be managed?
<--- Score

28. Have any additional benefits been identified that will result from closing all or most of the gaps?
<--- Score

29. What were the crucial 'moments of truth' on the process map?
<--- Score

30. Is data and process analysis, root cause analysis and quantifying the gap/opportunity in place?
<--- Score

31. What are evaluation criteria for the output?
<--- Score

32. Who is involved with workflow mapping?
<--- Score

33. What successful thing are you doing today that may be blinding you to new growth opportunities?
<--- Score

34. What are your outputs?
<--- Score

35. Did any value-added analysis or 'lean thinking' take place to identify some of the gaps shown on the 'as is' process map?
<--- Score

36. How is the way you as the leader think and process information affecting your organizational culture?
<--- Score

37. What other jobs or tasks affect the performance of the steps in the Business Cost Optimization process?
<--- Score

38. What internal processes need improvement?
<--- Score

39. How do you implement and manage your work processes to ensure that they meet design

requirements?

<--- Score

40. What Business Cost Optimization metrics are outputs of the process?

<--- Score

41. Did any additional data need to be collected?

<--- Score

42. Do quality systems drive continuous improvement?

<--- Score

43. What process should you select for improvement?

<--- Score

44. A compounding model resolution with available relevant data can often provide insight towards a solution methodology; which Business Cost Optimization models, tools and techniques are necessary?

<--- Score

45. What are the Business Cost Optimization design outputs?

<--- Score

46. Are you missing Business Cost Optimization opportunities?

<--- Score

47. What Business Cost Optimization data will be collected?

<--- Score

48. Do several people in different organizational units assist with the Business Cost Optimization process?

<--- Score

49. How is the data gathered?

<--- Score

50. Who is involved in the management review process?

<--- Score

51. What tools were used to narrow the list of possible causes?

<--- Score

52. What systems/processes must you excel at?

<--- Score

53. What qualifications are necessary?

<--- Score

54. What quality tools were used to get through the analyze phase?

<--- Score

55. Who will facilitate the team and process?

<--- Score

56. How do you identify specific Business Cost Optimization investment opportunities and emerging trends?

<--- Score

57. Was a cause-and-effect diagram used to explore the different types of causes (or sources of variation)?

<--- Score

58. What is the cost of poor quality as supported by the team's analysis?
<--- Score

59. What is the complexity of the output produced?
<--- Score

60. Think about the functions involved in your Business Cost Optimization project, what processes flow from these functions?
<--- Score

61. Who gets your output?
<--- Score

62. What data do you need to collect?
<--- Score

63. What qualifications are needed?
<--- Score

64. What are the revised rough estimates of the financial savings/opportunity for Business Cost Optimization improvements?
<--- Score

65. What are your current levels and trends in key measures or indicators of Business Cost Optimization product and process performance that are important to and directly serve your customers? How do these results compare with the performance of your competitors and other organizations with similar offerings?
<--- Score

66. Do you understand your management processes today?

<--- Score

67. Are Business Cost Optimization changes recognized early enough to be approved through the regular process?

<--- Score

68. What are your current levels and trends in key Business Cost Optimization measures or indicators of product and process performance that are important to and directly serve your customers?

<--- Score

69. Identify an operational issue in your organization, for example, could a particular task be done more quickly or more efficiently by Business Cost Optimization?

<--- Score

70. What are your key performance measures or indicators and in-process measures for the control and improvement of your Business Cost Optimization processes?

<--- Score

71. What Business Cost Optimization data should be collected?

<--- Score

72. What tools were used to generate the list of possible causes?

<--- Score

73. How will the Business Cost Optimization data be captured?
<--- Score

74. What is the Value Stream Mapping?
<--- Score

75. How are outputs preserved and protected?
<--- Score

76. How does the organization define, manage, and improve its Business Cost Optimization processes?
<--- Score

77. What did the team gain from developing a sub-process map?
<--- Score

78. How can risk management be tied procedurally to process elements?
<--- Score

79. Are your outputs consistent?
<--- Score

80. What other organizational variables, such as reward systems or communication systems, affect the performance of this Business Cost Optimization process?
<--- Score

81. What are the best opportunities for value improvement?
<--- Score

82. Has an output goal been set?

<--- Score

83. What qualifies as competition?
<--- Score

84. Is the performance gap determined?
<--- Score

85. What training and qualifications will you need?
<--- Score

86. How do you define collaboration and team output?
<--- Score

87. What Business Cost Optimization data should be managed?
<--- Score

88. Who will gather what data?
<--- Score

89. Have the problem and goal statements been updated to reflect the additional knowledge gained from the analyze phase?
<--- Score

90. Do your contracts/agreements contain data security obligations?
<--- Score

91. Is there any way to speed up the process?
<--- Score

92. What, related to, Business Cost Optimization processes does your organization outsource?

<--- Score

93. Were any designed experiments used to generate additional insight into the data analysis?
<--- Score

94. How many input/output points does it require?
<--- Score

95. What are the disruptive Business Cost Optimization technologies that enable your organization to radically change your business processes?
<--- Score

96. What are the necessary qualifications?
<--- Score

97. What data is gathered?
<--- Score

98. What output to create?
<--- Score

99. What does the data say about the performance of the stakeholder process?
<--- Score

100. What types of data do your Business Cost Optimization indicators require?
<--- Score

101. What is the Business Cost Optimization Driver?
<--- Score

102. What controls do you have in place to protect data?

<--- Score

103. Were there any improvement opportunities identified from the process analysis?

<--- Score

104. Is the final output clearly identified?

<--- Score

105. Where is the data coming from to measure compliance?

<--- Score

106. Have you defined which data is gathered how?

<--- Score

107. Who owns what data?

<--- Score

108. How do you use Business Cost Optimization data and information to support organizational decision making and innovation?

<--- Score

109. What qualifications and skills do you need?

<--- Score

110. What were the financial benefits resulting from any 'ground fruit or low-hanging fruit' (quick fixes)?

<--- Score

111. Is the gap/opportunity displayed and communicated in financial terms?

<--- Score

112. How often will data be collected for measures?
<--- Score

113. Is the required Business Cost Optimization data gathered?
<--- Score

114. Is there an established change management process?
<--- Score

115. Which Business Cost Optimization data should be retained?
<--- Score

116. Are gaps between current performance and the goal performance identified?
<--- Score

117. Do you have the authority to produce the output?
<--- Score

118. What are the personnel training and qualifications required?
<--- Score

119. What do you need to qualify?
<--- Score

120. What are the processes for audit reporting and management?
<--- Score

121. What is the oversight process?

<--- Score

122. How do you promote understanding that opportunity for improvement is not criticism of the status quo, or the people who created the status quo?
<--- Score

123. What are your best practices for minimizing Business Cost Optimization project risk, while demonstrating incremental value and quick wins throughout the Business Cost Optimization project lifecycle?
<--- Score

124. How do you measure the operational performance of your key work systems and processes, including productivity, cycle time, and other appropriate measures of process effectiveness, efficiency, and innovation?
<--- Score

125. What conclusions were drawn from the team's data collection and analysis? How did the team reach these conclusions?
<--- Score

126. What is the output?
<--- Score

127. How difficult is it to qualify what Business Cost Optimization ROI is?
<--- Score

128. Has data output been validated?
<--- Score

129. What process improvements will be needed?
<--- Score

130. Should you invest in industry-recognized qualifications?
<--- Score

Add up total points for this section:
_ _ _ _ _ = Total points for this section

Divided by: _ _ _ _ _ _ (number of statements answered) = _ _ _ _ _ _
Average score for this section

Transfer your score to the Business Cost Optimization Index at the beginning of the Self-Assessment.

CRITERION #5: IMPROVE:

INTENT: Develop a practical solution. Innovate, establish and test the solution and to measure the results.

In my belief, the answer to this question is clearly defined:

5 Strongly Agree

4 Agree

3 Neutral

2 Disagree

1 Strongly Disagree

1. Where do you need Business Cost Optimization improvement?
<--- Score

2. How do you measure improved Business Cost Optimization service perception, and satisfaction?
<--- Score

3. When you map the key players in your own work

and the types/domains of relationships with them, which relationships do you find easy and which challenging, and why?

<--- Score

4. How do you improve Business Cost Optimization service perception, and satisfaction?

<--- Score

5. Are the most efficient solutions problem-specific?

<--- Score

6. If you could go back in time five years, what decision would you make differently? What is your best guess as to what decision you're making today you might regret five years from now?

<--- Score

7. What were the underlying assumptions on the cost-benefit analysis?

<--- Score

8. How do you go about comparing Business Cost Optimization approaches/solutions?

<--- Score

9. Do you have the optimal project management team structure?

<--- Score

10. Is the Business Cost Optimization solution sustainable?

<--- Score

11. Is any Business Cost Optimization documentation required?

<--- Score

12. How will you know that a change is an improvement?
<--- Score

13. Risk factors: what are the characteristics of Business Cost Optimization that make it risky?
<--- Score

14. Is supporting Business Cost Optimization documentation required?
<--- Score

15. Is risk periodically assessed?
<--- Score

16. At what point will vulnerability assessments be performed once Business Cost Optimization is put into production (e.g., ongoing Risk Management after implementation)?
<--- Score

17. Who will be responsible for making the decisions to include or exclude requested changes once Business Cost Optimization is underway?
<--- Score

18. What communications are necessary to support the implementation of the solution?
<--- Score

19. Which of the recognised risks out of all risks can be most likely transferred?
<--- Score

20. What are the expected Business Cost Optimization results?
<--- Score

21. Was a pilot designed for the proposed solution(s)?
<--- Score

22. Who will be using the results of the measurement activities?
<--- Score

23. How significant is the improvement in the eyes of the end user?
<--- Score

24. To what extent does management recognize Business Cost Optimization as a tool to increase the results?
<--- Score

25. How are policy decisions made and where?
<--- Score

26. For decision problems, how do you develop a decision statement?
<--- Score

27. Risk events: what are the things that could go wrong?
<--- Score

28. Where do the Business Cost Optimization decisions reside?
<--- Score

29. How do you manage and improve your Business

Cost Optimization work systems to deliver customer value and achieve organizational success and sustainability?

<--- Score

30. What actually has to improve and by how much?

<--- Score

31. Who will be responsible for documenting the Business Cost Optimization requirements in detail?

<--- Score

32. Can the solution be designed and implemented within an acceptable time period?

<--- Score

33. How do you define the solutions' scope?

<--- Score

34. For estimation problems, how do you develop an estimation statement?

<--- Score

35. Is pilot data collected and analyzed?

<--- Score

36. Does the goal represent a desired result that can be measured?

<--- Score

37. Is the implementation plan designed?

<--- Score

38. Are procedures documented for managing Business Cost Optimization risks?

<--- Score

39. How are Business Cost Optimization risks managed?
<--- Score

40. Is there a high likelihood that any recommendations will achieve their intended results?
<--- Score

41. How risky is your organization?
<--- Score

42. Are risk management tasks balanced centrally and locally?
<--- Score

43. Have you identified breakpoints and/or risk tolerances that will trigger broad consideration of a potential need for intervention or modification of strategy?
<--- Score

44. Is the Business Cost Optimization risk managed?
<--- Score

45. How can you improve performance?
<--- Score

46. What are the concrete Business Cost Optimization results?
<--- Score

47. What is the magnitude of the improvements?
<--- Score

48. Was a Business Cost Optimization charter

developed?
<--- Score

49. How can you better manage risk?
<--- Score

50. How scalable is your Business Cost Optimization solution?
<--- Score

51. What area needs the greatest improvement?
<--- Score

52. Do you combine technical expertise with business knowledge and Business Cost Optimization Key topics include lifecycles, development approaches, requirements and how to make a business case?
<--- Score

53. Are the key business and technology risks being managed?
<--- Score

54. Who controls key decisions that will be made?
<--- Score

55. What error proofing will be done to address some of the discrepancies observed in the 'as is' process?
<--- Score

56. Is the measure of success for Business Cost Optimization understandable to a variety of people?
<--- Score

57. Is there a cost/benefit analysis of optimal

solution(s)?
<--- Score

58. Is there a small-scale pilot for proposed improvement(s)? What conclusions were drawn from the outcomes of a pilot?
<--- Score

59. Are you assessing Business Cost Optimization and risk?
<--- Score

60. Who controls the risk?
<--- Score

61. Who manages Business Cost Optimization risk?
<--- Score

62. Why improve in the first place?
<--- Score

63. How can you improve Business Cost Optimization?
<--- Score

64. Who are the key stakeholders for the Business Cost Optimization evaluation?
<--- Score

65. What resources are required for the improvement efforts?
<--- Score

66. What is Business Cost Optimization risk?
<--- Score

67. Can you identify any significant risks or exposures to Business Cost Optimization third-parties (vendors, service providers, alliance partners etc) that concern you?
<--- Score

68. What lessons, if any, from a pilot were incorporated into the design of the full-scale solution?
<--- Score

69. How do you improve your likelihood of success ?
<--- Score

70. What are the Business Cost Optimization security risks?
<--- Score

71. Is a solution implementation plan established, including schedule/work breakdown structure, resources, risk management plan, cost/budget, and control plan?
<--- Score

72. Are risk triggers captured?
<--- Score

73. Have you achieved Business Cost Optimization improvements?
<--- Score

74. How do you improve productivity?
<--- Score

75. Would you develop a Business Cost Optimization Communication Strategy?
<--- Score

76. How do you mitigate Business Cost Optimization risk?
<--- Score

77. What is the risk?
<--- Score

78. Were any criteria developed to assist the team in testing and evaluating potential solutions?
<--- Score

79. How will you measure the results?
<--- Score

80. What attendant changes will need to be made to ensure that the solution is successful?
<--- Score

81. What does the 'should be' process map/design look like?
<--- Score

82. What tools do you use once you have decided on a Business Cost Optimization strategy and more importantly how do you choose?
<--- Score

83. How do you measure progress and evaluate training effectiveness?
<--- Score

84. How will you recognize and celebrate results?
<--- Score

85. Do vendor agreements bring new compliance risk

?
<--- Score

86. Do you cover the five essential competencies: Communication, Collaboration,Innovation, Adaptability, and Leadership that improve an organizations ability to leverage the new Business Cost Optimization in a volatile global economy?
<--- Score

87. How does your organization evaluate strategic Business Cost Optimization success?
<--- Score

88. Who do you report Business Cost Optimization results to?
<--- Score

89. What is the team's contingency plan for potential problems occurring in implementation?
<--- Score

90. What strategies for Business Cost Optimization improvement are successful?
<--- Score

91. What assumptions are made about the solution and approach?
<--- Score

92. How do you link measurement and risk?
<--- Score

93. How can skill-level changes improve Business Cost Optimization?
<--- Score

94. Who manages supplier risk management in your organization?

<--- Score

95. Are the risks fully understood, reasonable and manageable?

<--- Score

96. Is there any other Business Cost Optimization solution?

<--- Score

97. How risky is your organization?

<--- Score

98. What do you want to improve?

<--- Score

99. What tools were most useful during the improve phase?

<--- Score

100. How do you manage Business Cost Optimization risk?

<--- Score

101. Risk Identification: What are the possible risk events your organization faces in relation to Business Cost Optimization?

<--- Score

102. Are decisions made in a timely manner?

<--- Score

103. What risks do you need to manage?

<--- Score

104. What are the affordable Business Cost Optimization risks?
<--- Score

105. What to do with the results or outcomes of measurements?
<--- Score

106. What is the Business Cost Optimization's sustainability risk?
<--- Score

107. Explorations of the frontiers of Business Cost Optimization will help you build influence, improve Business Cost Optimization, optimize decision making, and sustain change, what is your approach?
<--- Score

108. Who are the Business Cost Optimization decision-makers?
<--- Score

109. What Business Cost Optimization improvements can be made?
<--- Score

110. What tools were used to evaluate the potential solutions?
<--- Score

111. Will the controls trigger any other risks?
<--- Score

112. How do you decide how much to remunerate an employee?
<--- Score

113. How will you know that you have improved?
<--- Score

114. What improvements have been achieved?
<--- Score

115. What should a proof of concept or pilot accomplish?
<--- Score

116. Who are the Business Cost Optimization decision makers?
<--- Score

117. What went well, what should change, what can improve?
<--- Score

118. In the past few months, what is the smallest change you have made that has had the biggest positive result? What was it about that small change that produced the large return?
<--- Score

119. Do you need to do a usability evaluation?
<--- Score

120. Is the scope clearly documented?
<--- Score

121. How will you know when its improved?
<--- Score

122. How do you deal with Business Cost Optimization risk?
<--- Score

123. How do the Business Cost Optimization results compare with the performance of your competitors and other organizations with similar offerings?
<--- Score

124. What is Business Cost Optimization's impact on utilizing the best solution(s)?
<--- Score

125. What tools were used to tap into the creativity and encourage 'outside the box' thinking?
<--- Score

126. Who should make the Business Cost Optimization decisions?
<--- Score

127. What practices helps your organization to develop its capacity to recognize patterns?
<--- Score

128. Is the Business Cost Optimization documentation thorough?
<--- Score

129. What can you do to improve?
<--- Score

130. What criteria will you use to assess your Business Cost Optimization risks?
<--- Score

131. What is the implementation plan?
<--- Score

132. Is the optimal solution selected based on testing and analysis?
<--- Score

133. Business Cost Optimization risk decisions: whose call Is It?
<--- Score

134. Who are the people involved in developing and implementing Business Cost Optimization?
<--- Score

135. What are your current levels and trends in key measures or indicators of workforce and leader development?
<--- Score

136. How is knowledge sharing about risk management improved?
<--- Score

137. Do those selected for the Business Cost Optimization team have a good general understanding of what Business Cost Optimization is all about?
<--- Score

138. What needs improvement? Why?
<--- Score

139. Which Business Cost Optimization solution is appropriate?

<--- Score

140. How do you measure risk?
<--- Score

Add up total points for this section:
_ _ _ _ _ = Total points for this section

Divided by: _ _ _ _ _ _ (number of
statements answered) = _ _ _ _ _ _
Average score for this section

Transfer your score to the Business Cost
Optimization Index at the beginning of
the Self-Assessment.

CRITERION #6: CONTROL:

INTENT: Implement the practical solution. Maintain the performance and correct possible complications.

In my belief, the answer to this question is clearly defined:

5 Strongly Agree

4 Agree

3 Neutral

2 Disagree

1 Strongly Disagree

1. What do your reports reflect?
<--- Score

2. How will the process owner and team be able to hold the gains?
<--- Score

3. Does Business Cost Optimization appropriately measure and monitor risk?

<--- Score

4. Who is the Business Cost Optimization process owner?
<--- Score

5. Are there documented procedures?
<--- Score

6. What is your plan to assess your security risks?
<--- Score

7. Is reporting being used or needed?
<--- Score

8. Do you monitor the Business Cost Optimization decisions made and fine tune them as they evolve?
<--- Score

9. In the case of a Business Cost Optimization project, the criteria for the audit derive from implementation objectives, an audit of a Business Cost Optimization project involves assessing whether the recommendations outlined for implementation have been met, can you track that any Business Cost Optimization project is implemented as planned, and is it working?
<--- Score

10. Will any special training be provided for results interpretation?
<--- Score

11. What should the next improvement project be that is related to Business Cost Optimization?
<--- Score

12. Is there a transfer of ownership and knowledge to process owner and process team tasked with the responsibilities.
<--- Score

13. How is change control managed?
<--- Score

14. How widespread is its use?
<--- Score

15. How will you measure your QA plan's effectiveness?
<--- Score

16. What are you attempting to measure/monitor?
<--- Score

17. How might the group capture best practices and lessons learned so as to leverage improvements?
<--- Score

18. Do the Business Cost Optimization decisions you make today help people and the planet tomorrow?
<--- Score

19. What is the control/monitoring plan?
<--- Score

20. What adjustments to the strategies are needed?
<--- Score

21. What can you control?
<--- Score

22. Who sets the Business Cost Optimization standards?
<--- Score

23. Is a response plan in place for when the input, process, or output measures indicate an 'out-of-control' condition?
<--- Score

24. Does the Business Cost Optimization performance meet the customer's requirements?
<--- Score

25. Do the viable solutions scale to future needs?
<--- Score

26. How do you monitor usage and cost?
<--- Score

27. How do you select, collect, align, and integrate Business Cost Optimization data and information for tracking daily operations and overall organizational performance, including progress relative to strategic objectives and action plans?
<--- Score

28. Does the response plan contain a definite closed loop continual improvement scheme (e.g., plan-do-check-act)?
<--- Score

29. How likely is the current Business Cost Optimization plan to come in on schedule or on budget?
<--- Score

30. Does a troubleshooting guide exist or is it needed?
<--- Score

31. Can you adapt and adjust to changing Business Cost Optimization situations?
<--- Score

32. Who controls critical resources?
<--- Score

33. What other systems, operations, processes, and infrastructures (hiring practices, staffing, training, incentives/rewards, metrics/dashboards/scorecards, etc.) need updates, additions, changes, or deletions in order to facilitate knowledge transfer and improvements?
<--- Score

34. Is there a documented and implemented monitoring plan?
<--- Score

35. Who is going to spread your message?
<--- Score

36. What is the recommended frequency of auditing?
<--- Score

37. Are pertinent alerts monitored, analyzed and distributed to appropriate personnel?
<--- Score

38. What are your results for key measures or indicators of the accomplishment of your Business Cost Optimization strategy and action plans, including

building and strengthening core competencies?
<--- Score

39. How will new or emerging customer needs/ requirements be checked/communicated to orient the process toward meeting the new specifications and continually reducing variation?
<--- Score

40. Will your goals reflect your program budget?
<--- Score

41. How will the process owner verify improvement in present and future sigma levels, process capabilities?
<--- Score

42. What is the standard for acceptable Business Cost Optimization performance?
<--- Score

43. What Business Cost Optimization standards are applicable?
<--- Score

44. Is there a Business Cost Optimization Communication plan covering who needs to get what information when?
<--- Score

45. How will input, process, and output variables be checked to detect for sub-optimal conditions?
<--- Score

46. How can you best use all of your knowledge repositories to enhance learning and sharing?
<--- Score

47. What are the known security controls?
<--- Score

48. Is there a recommended audit plan for routine surveillance inspections of Business Cost Optimization's gains?
<--- Score

49. What quality tools were useful in the control phase?
<--- Score

50. Where do ideas that reach policy makers and planners as proposals for Business Cost Optimization strengthening and reform actually originate?
<--- Score

51. How do you plan for the cost of succession?
<--- Score

52. Is there documentation that will support the successful operation of the improvement?
<--- Score

53. Is there a standardized process?
<--- Score

54. What is your theory of human motivation, and how does your compensation plan fit with that view?
<--- Score

55. Act/Adjust: What Do you Need to Do Differently?
<--- Score

56. Are documented procedures clear and easy to follow for the operators?
<--- Score

57. Has the Business Cost Optimization value of standards been quantified?
<--- Score

58. How will report readings be checked to effectively monitor performance?
<--- Score

59. Has the improved process and its steps been standardized?
<--- Score

60. Is there a control plan in place for sustaining improvements (short and long-term)?
<--- Score

61. What other areas of the group might benefit from the Business Cost Optimization team's improvements, knowledge, and learning?
<--- Score

62. Is the Business Cost Optimization test/monitoring cost justified?
<--- Score

63. Do you monitor the effectiveness of your Business Cost Optimization activities?
<--- Score

64. Are the planned controls working?
<--- Score

65. Is new knowledge gained imbedded in the response plan?

<--- Score

66. How do your controls stack up?

<--- Score

67. What are the key elements of your Business Cost Optimization performance improvement system, including your evaluation, organizational learning, and innovation processes?

<--- Score

68. What is the best design framework for Business Cost Optimization organization now that, in a post industrial-age if the top-down, command and control model is no longer relevant?

<--- Score

69. Is knowledge gained on process shared and institutionalized?

<--- Score

70. Who will be in control?

<--- Score

71. How do you plan on providing proper recognition and disclosure of supporting companies?

<--- Score

72. How will the day-to-day responsibilities for monitoring and continual improvement be transferred from the improvement team to the process owner?

<--- Score

73. Who has control over resources?
<--- Score

74. Are operating procedures consistent?
<--- Score

75. Will the team be available to assist members in planning investigations?
<--- Score

76. Are new process steps, standards, and documentation ingrained into normal operations?
<--- Score

77. What do you stand for--and what are you against?
<--- Score

78. How is Business Cost Optimization project cost planned, managed, monitored?
<--- Score

79. What are the critical parameters to watch?
<--- Score

80. Are the Business Cost Optimization standards challenging?
<--- Score

81. How do controls support value?
<--- Score

82. How do you spread information?
<--- Score

83. Have new or revised work instructions resulted?
<--- Score

84. What key inputs and outputs are being measured on an ongoing basis?
<--- Score

85. How will Business Cost Optimization decisions be made and monitored?
<--- Score

86. What are customers monitoring?
<--- Score

87. What should you measure to verify efficiency gains?
<--- Score

88. Is there an action plan in case of emergencies?
<--- Score

89. Does job training on the documented procedures need to be part of the process team's education and training?
<--- Score

90. How do you establish and deploy modified action plans if circumstances require a shift in plans and rapid execution of new plans?
<--- Score

91. How do you encourage people to take control and responsibility?
<--- Score

92. Implementation Planning: is a pilot needed to test

the changes before a full roll out occurs?
<--- Score

93. What are the performance and scale of the Business Cost Optimization tools?
<--- Score

94. Are suggested corrective/restorative actions indicated on the response plan for known causes to problems that might surface?
<--- Score

95. Is a response plan established and deployed?
<--- Score

96. Are you measuring, monitoring and predicting Business Cost Optimization activities to optimize operations and profitability, and enhancing outcomes?
<--- Score

97. Against what alternative is success being measured?
<--- Score

Add up total points for this section:
_ _ _ _ _ = Total points for this section

Divided by: _ _ _ _ _ _ (number of statements answered) = _ _ _ _ _ _
Average score for this section

Transfer your score to the Business Cost Optimization Index at the beginning of the Self-Assessment.

CRITERION #7: SUSTAIN:

INTENT: Retain the benefits.

In my belief, the answer to this
question is clearly defined:

5 Strongly Agree

4 Agree

3 Neutral

2 Disagree

1 Strongly Disagree

1. How much contingency will be available in the
budget?
<--- Score

2. How do you foster the skills, knowledge, talents,
attributes, and characteristics you want to have?
<--- Score

3. Marketing budgets are tighter, consumers are more
skeptical, and social media has changed forever the
way we talk about Business Cost Optimization, how

do you gain traction?
<--- Score

4. Whose voice (department, ethnic group, women, older workers, etc) might you have missed hearing from in your company, and how might you amplify this voice to create positive momentum for your business?
<--- Score

5. How are you doing compared to your industry?
<--- Score

6. What counts that you are not counting?
<--- Score

7. If you find that you havent accomplished one of the goals for one of the steps of the Business Cost Optimization strategy, what will you do to fix it?
<--- Score

8. What stupid rule would you most like to kill?
<--- Score

9. What must you excel at?
<--- Score

10. Have benefits been optimized with all key stakeholders?
<--- Score

11. Do you know what you are doing? And who do you call if you don't?
<--- Score

12. Who do we want your customers to become?

<--- Score

13. What is your formula for success in Business Cost Optimization ?
<--- Score

14. How do you deal with Business Cost Optimization changes?
<--- Score

15. Who do you think the world wants your organization to be?
<--- Score

16. Is Business Cost Optimization dependent on the successful delivery of a current project?
<--- Score

17. Are you changing as fast as the world around you?
<--- Score

18. Who will be responsible for deciding whether Business Cost Optimization goes ahead or not after the initial investigations?
<--- Score

19. What have been your experiences in defining long range Business Cost Optimization goals?
<--- Score

20. To whom do you add value?
<--- Score

21. Do you think Business Cost Optimization accomplishes the goals you expect it to accomplish?

<--- Score

22. Do you feel that more should be done in the Business Cost Optimization area?
<--- Score

23. What knowledge, skills and characteristics mark a good Business Cost Optimization project manager?
<--- Score

24. Are the assumptions believable and achievable?
<--- Score

25. What business benefits will Business Cost Optimization goals deliver if achieved?
<--- Score

26. What are you trying to prove to yourself, and how might it be hijacking your life and business success?
<--- Score

27. What are the barriers to increased Business Cost Optimization production?
<--- Score

28. What is your BATNA (best alternative to a negotiated agreement)?
<--- Score

29. What are the challenges?
<--- Score

30. How do customers see your organization?
<--- Score

31. Why is it important to have senior management support for a Business Cost Optimization project?
<--- Score

32. Why is Business Cost Optimization important for you now?
<--- Score

33. Is there any existing Business Cost Optimization governance structure?
<--- Score

34. Why will customers want to buy your organizations products/services?
<--- Score

35. Who have you, as a company, historically been when you've been at your best?
<--- Score

36. Whom among your colleagues do you trust, and for what?
<--- Score

37. In retrospect, of the projects that you pulled the plug on, what percent do you wish had been allowed to keep going, and what percent do you wish had ended earlier?
<--- Score

38. What is your Business Cost Optimization strategy?
<--- Score

39. Are you paying enough attention to the partners your company depends on to succeed?
<--- Score

40. How do you assess the Business Cost Optimization pitfalls that are inherent in implementing it?
<--- Score

41. How do you set Business Cost Optimization stretch targets and how do you get people to not only participate in setting these stretch targets but also that they strive to achieve these?
<--- Score

42. Which functions and people interact with the supplier and or customer?
<--- Score

43. Has implementation been effective in reaching specified objectives so far?
<--- Score

44. How can you negotiate Business Cost Optimization successfully with a stubborn boss, an irate client, or a deceitful coworker?
<--- Score

45. Who else should you help?
<--- Score

46. What projects are going on in the organization today, and what resources are those projects using from the resource pools?
<--- Score

47. What are the business goals Business Cost Optimization is aiming to achieve?
<--- Score

48. How do you listen to customers to obtain actionable information?
<--- Score

49. What trophy do you want on your mantle?
<--- Score

50. What goals did you miss?
<--- Score

51. Will there be any necessary staff changes (redundancies or new hires)?
<--- Score

52. How do you maintain Business Cost Optimization's Integrity?
<--- Score

53. If your company went out of business tomorrow, would anyone who doesn't get a paycheck here care?
<--- Score

54. What may be the consequences for the performance of an organization if all stakeholders are not consulted regarding Business Cost Optimization?
<--- Score

55. What will be the consequences to the stakeholder (financial, reputation etc) if Business Cost Optimization does not go ahead or fails to deliver the objectives?
<--- Score

56. Who is on the team?
<--- Score

57. Is your strategy driving your strategy? Or is the way in which you allocate resources driving your strategy?
<--- Score

58. What was the last experiment you ran?
<--- Score

59. What management system can you use to leverage the Business Cost Optimization experience, ideas, and concerns of the people closest to the work to be done?
<--- Score

60. How likely is it that a customer would recommend your company to a friend or colleague?
<--- Score

61. Do you say no to customers for no reason?
<--- Score

62. Is maximizing Business Cost Optimization protection the same as minimizing Business Cost Optimization loss?
<--- Score

63. If your customer were your grandmother, would you tell her to buy what you're selling?
<--- Score

64. Which models, tools and techniques are necessary?
<--- Score

65. Would you rather sell to knowledgeable and

informed customers or to uninformed customers?
<--- Score

66. Are you satisfied with your current role? If not, what is missing from it?
<--- Score

67. Are you making progress, and are you making progress as Business Cost Optimization leaders?
<--- Score

68. Are your responses positive or negative?
<--- Score

69. Is your basic point _____ or _____?
<--- Score

70. Who are four people whose careers you have enhanced?
<--- Score

71. Were lessons learned captured and communicated?
<--- Score

72. How do you transition from the baseline to the target?
<--- Score

73. What is an unauthorized commitment?
<--- Score

74. If no one would ever find out about your accomplishments, how would you lead differently?
<--- Score

75. What are current Business Cost Optimization paradigms?
<--- Score

76. Is a Business Cost Optimization breakthrough on the horizon?
<--- Score

77. What is the overall business strategy?
<--- Score

78. How do senior leaders deploy your organizations vision and values through your leadership system, to the workforce, to key suppliers and partners, and to customers and other stakeholders, as appropriate?
<--- Score

79. If you had to leave your organization for a year and the only communication you could have with employees/colleagues was a single paragraph, what would you write?
<--- Score

80. Do you see more potential in people than they do in themselves?
<--- Score

81. Will it be accepted by users?
<--- Score

82. Who are the key stakeholders?
<--- Score

83. What have you done to protect your business from competitive encroachment?
<--- Score

84. Are new benefits received and understood?
<--- Score

85. What is the craziest thing you can do?
<--- Score

86. How long will it take to change?
<--- Score

87. Which individuals, teams or departments will be involved in Business Cost Optimization?
<--- Score

88. Why do and why don't your customers like your organization?
<--- Score

89. How do you govern and fulfill your societal responsibilities?
<--- Score

90. Instead of going to current contacts for new ideas, what if you reconnected with dormant contacts-- the people you used to know? If you were going reactivate a dormant tie, who would it be?
<--- Score

91. Do you have the right capabilities and capacities?
<--- Score

92. Who is responsible for ensuring appropriate resources (time, people and money) are allocated to Business Cost Optimization?
<--- Score

93. How important is Business Cost Optimization to the user organizations mission?

<--- Score

94. If you got fired and a new hire took your place, what would she do different?

<--- Score

95. At what moment would you think; Will I get fired?

<--- Score

96. Where can you break convention?

<--- Score

97. What happens when a new employee joins the organization?

<--- Score

98. What you are going to do to affect the numbers?

<--- Score

99. How will you motivate the stakeholders with the least vested interest?

<--- Score

100. What is the recommended frequency of auditing?

<--- Score

101. What are strategies for increasing support and reducing opposition?

<--- Score

102. What is the purpose of Business Cost Optimization in relation to the mission?

<--- Score

103. What do we do when new problems arise?
<--- Score

104. What is the range of capabilities?
<--- Score

105. How much does Business Cost Optimization help?
<--- Score

106. Are all key stakeholders present at all Structured Walkthroughs?
<--- Score

107. What are the potential basics of Business Cost Optimization fraud?
<--- Score

108. Can you maintain your growth without detracting from the factors that have contributed to your success?
<--- Score

109. If you do not follow, then how to lead?
<--- Score

110. What are the success criteria that will indicate that Business Cost Optimization objectives have been met and the benefits delivered?
<--- Score

111. Are you using a design thinking approach and integrating Innovation, Business Cost Optimization Experience, and Brand Value?

<--- Score

112. What is the big Business Cost Optimization idea?
<--- Score

113. What is effective Business Cost Optimization?
<--- Score

114. Is a Business Cost Optimization team work effort in place?
<--- Score

115. How do you create buy-in?
<--- Score

116. What is the kind of project structure that would be appropriate for your Business Cost Optimization project, should it be formal and complex, or can it be less formal and relatively simple?
<--- Score

117. Is the impact that Business Cost Optimization has shown?
<--- Score

118. Are you relevant? Will you be relevant five years from now? Ten?
<--- Score

119. In the past year, what have you done (or could you have done) to increase the accurate perception of your company/brand as ethical and honest?
<--- Score

120. How do you cross-sell and up-sell your

Business Cost Optimization success?

<--- Score

121. How does Business Cost Optimization integrate with other stakeholder initiatives?

<--- Score

122. When information truly is ubiquitous, when reach and connectivity are completely global, when computing resources are infinite, and when a whole new set of impossibilities are not only possible, but happening, what will that do to your business?

<--- Score

123. What are the key enablers to make this Business Cost Optimization move?

<--- Score

124. What are your personal philosophies regarding Business Cost Optimization and how do they influence your work?

<--- Score

125. Political -is anyone trying to undermine this project?

<--- Score

126. Why not do Business Cost Optimization?

<--- Score

127. What role does communication play in the success or failure of a Business Cost Optimization project?

<--- Score

128. What threat is Business Cost Optimization

addressing?

<--- Score

129. How do you keep the momentum going?

<--- Score

130. What are specific Business Cost Optimization rules to follow?

<--- Score

131. What unique value proposition (UVP) do you offer?

<--- Score

132. How do you manage Business Cost Optimization Knowledge Management (KM)?

<--- Score

133. Who uses your product in ways you never expected?

<--- Score

134. Have new benefits been realized?

<--- Score

135. How do you lead with Business Cost Optimization in mind?

<--- Score

136. What could happen if you do not do it?

<--- Score

137. Is there any reason to believe the opposite of my current belief?

<--- Score

138. What are the rules and assumptions your industry operates under? What if the opposite were true?
<--- Score

139. What are the long-term Business Cost Optimization goals?
<--- Score

140. If you weren't already in this business, would you enter it today? And if not, what are you going to do about it?
<--- Score

141. What potential megatrends could make your business model obsolete?
<--- Score

142. Who, on the executive team or the board, has spoken to a customer recently?
<--- Score

143. Who is responsible for Business Cost Optimization?
<--- Score

144. What is a feasible sequencing of reform initiatives over time?
<--- Score

145. How will you insure seamless interoperability of Business Cost Optimization moving forward?
<--- Score

146. How can you become more high-tech but still be high touch?
<--- Score

147. What one word do you want to own in the minds of your customers, employees, and partners?
<--- Score

148. Why should people listen to you?
<--- Score

149. What new services of functionality will be implemented next with Business Cost Optimization ?
<--- Score

150. Can the schedule be done in the given time?
<--- Score

151. Why should you adopt a Business Cost Optimization framework?
<--- Score

152. How do you know if you are successful?
<--- Score

153. What does your signature ensure?
<--- Score

154. How do you foster innovation?
<--- Score

155. What are the top 3 things at the forefront of your Business Cost Optimization agendas for the next 3 years?
<--- Score

156. Do you have the right people on the bus?

<--- Score

157. Ask yourself: how would you do this work if you only had one staff member to do it?
<--- Score

158. How do you accomplish your long range Business Cost Optimization goals?
<--- Score

159. Who do you want your customers to become?
<--- Score

160. What did you miss in the interview for the worst hire you ever made?
<--- Score

161. Who will determine interim and final deadlines?
<--- Score

162. What happens at your organization when people fail?
<--- Score

163. How do you provide a safe environment -physically and emotionally?
<--- Score

164. How can you become the company that would put you out of business?
<--- Score

165. How do you keep records, of what?
<--- Score

166. What are the essentials of internal Business Cost

Optimization management?

<--- Score

167. What are you challenging?

<--- Score

168. Is there a work around that you can use?

<--- Score

169. What happens if you do not have enough funding?

<--- Score

170. How can you incorporate support to ensure safe and effective use of Business Cost Optimization into the services that you provide?

<--- Score

171. Do you think you know, or do you know you know ?

<--- Score

172. Are you / should you be revolutionary or evolutionary?

<--- Score

173. Who is the main stakeholder, with ultimate responsibility for driving Business Cost Optimization forward?

<--- Score

174. How do you track customer value, profitability or financial return, organizational success, and sustainability?

<--- Score

175. Can you do all this work?
<--- Score

176. How do you ensure that implementations of Business Cost Optimization products are done in a way that ensures safety?
<--- Score

177. What relationships among Business Cost Optimization trends do you perceive?
<--- Score

178. Who is responsible for errors?
<--- Score

179. Who will manage the integration of tools?
<--- Score

180. How is implementation research currently incorporated into each of your goals?
<--- Score

181. What is your question? Why?
<--- Score

182. Did your employees make progress today?
<--- Score

183. What Business Cost Optimization modifications can you make work for you?
<--- Score

184. Do you have an implicit bias for capital investments over people investments?
<--- Score

185. What is it like to work for you?
<--- Score

186. How will you ensure you get what you expected?
<--- Score

187. What would you recommend your friend do if he/she were facing this dilemma?
<--- Score

188. Do you know who is a friend or a foe?
<--- Score

189. What is the funding source for this project?
<--- Score

190. Are you maintaining a past–present–future perspective throughout the Business Cost Optimization discussion?
<--- Score

191. What is the source of the strategies for Business Cost Optimization strengthening and reform?
<--- Score

192. What trouble can you get into?
<--- Score

193. Who will provide the final approval of Business Cost Optimization deliverables?
<--- Score

194. What Business Cost Optimization skills are most important?
<--- Score

195. How do you determine the key elements that affect Business Cost Optimization workforce satisfaction, how are these elements determined for different workforce groups and segments?
<--- Score

196. What are the short and long-term Business Cost Optimization goals?
<--- Score

197. How do you engage the workforce, in addition to satisfying them?
<--- Score

198. Do you have enough freaky customers in your portfolio pushing you to the limit day in and day out?
<--- Score

199. How do you go about securing Business Cost Optimization?
<--- Score

200. How do you stay inspired?
<--- Score

201. Are the criteria for selecting recommendations stated?
<--- Score

202. Think of your Business Cost Optimization project, what are the main functions?
<--- Score

203. Which Business Cost Optimization goals are the most important?
<--- Score

204. What are the usability implications of Business Cost Optimization actions?
<--- Score

205. How will you know that the Business Cost Optimization project has been successful?
<--- Score

206. How do you proactively clarify deliverables and Business Cost Optimization quality expectations?
<--- Score

207. What is the estimated value of the project?
<--- Score

208. What would have to be true for the option on the table to be the best possible choice?
<--- Score

209. Are there any activities that you can take off your to do list?
<--- Score

210. Who are your customers?
<--- Score

211. Is it economical; do you have the time and money?
<--- Score

212. What are your most important goals for the strategic Business Cost Optimization objectives?
<--- Score

213. How do you make it meaningful in connecting

Business Cost Optimization with what users do day-to-day?

<--- Score

214. Is the Business Cost Optimization organization completing tasks effectively and efficiently?

<--- Score

215. Operational - will it work?

<--- Score

216. If you were responsible for initiating and implementing major changes in your organization, what steps might you take to ensure acceptance of those changes?

<--- Score

217. What is your competitive advantage?

<--- Score

218. Is Business Cost Optimization realistic, or are you setting yourself up for failure?

<--- Score

219. Do Business Cost Optimization rules make a reasonable demand on a users capabilities?

<--- Score

220. In a project to restructure Business Cost Optimization outcomes, which stakeholders would you involve?

<--- Score

Add up total points for this section:

_ _ _ _ _ = Total points for this section

Divided by: _ _ _ _ _ _ (number of
statements answered) = _ _ _ _ _ _
Average score for this section

Transfer your score to the Business Cost
Optimization Index at the beginning of
the Self-Assessment.

Business Cost Optimization and Managing Projects, Criteria for Project Managers:

1.0 Initiating Process Group: Business Cost Optimization

1. What are the short and long term implications?

2. Were decisions made in a timely manner?

3. Do you understand all business (operational), technical, resource and vendor risks associated with the Business Cost Optimization project?

4. Who are the Business Cost Optimization project stakeholders?

5. What are the constraints?

6. What do you need to do?

7. If the risk event occurs, what will you do?

8. Do you know all the stakeholders impacted by the Business Cost Optimization project and what needs are?

9. What were things that you did very well and want to do the same again on the next Business Cost Optimization project?

10. Which of six sigmas dmaic phases focuses on the measurement of internal process that affect factors that are critical to quality?

11. The Business Cost Optimization project you are managing has nine stakeholders. How many channel of communications are there between corresponding

stakeholders?

12. Have the stakeholders identified all individual requirements pertaining to business process?

13. What were the challenges that you encountered during the execution of a previous Business Cost Optimization project that you would not want to repeat?

14. Are there resources to maintain and support the outcome of the Business Cost Optimization project?

15. What were things that you need to improve?

16. Who is performing the work of the Business Cost Optimization project?

17. At which cmmi level are software processes documented, standardized, and integrated into a standard to-be practiced process for your organization?

18. Although the Business Cost Optimization project manager does not directly manage procurement and contracting activities, who does manage procurement and contracting activities in your organization then if not the PM?

19. What are the overarching issues of your organization?

20. What communication items need improvement?

1.1 Project Charter: Business Cost Optimization

21. What material?

22. What metrics could you look at?

23. Customer benefits: what customer requirements does this Business Cost Optimization project address?

24. When?

25. Is it an improvement over existing products?

26. Major high-level milestone targets: what events measure progress?

27. Who ise input and support will this Business Cost Optimization project require?

28. What are some examples of a business case?

29. Will this replace an existing product?

30. What is the business need?

31. What is the purpose of the Business Cost Optimization project?

32. Why is a Business Cost Optimization project Charter used?

33. Are you building in-house ?

34. How do you manage integration?

35. What goes into your Business Cost Optimization project Charter?

36. Assumptions: what factors, for planning purposes, are you considering to be true?

37. What date will the task finish?

38. Does the Business Cost Optimization project need to consider any special capacity or capability issues?

39. How high should you set your goals?

40. What outcome, in measureable terms, are you hoping to accomplish?

1.2 Stakeholder Register: Business Cost Optimization

41. How big is the gap?

42. How will reports be created?

43. How much influence do they have on the Business Cost Optimization project?

44. Is your organization ready for change?

45. How should employers make voices heard?

46. What is the power of the stakeholder?

47. What opportunities exist to provide communications?

48. Who are the stakeholders?

49. Who is managing stakeholder engagement?

50. What & Why?

51. Who wants to talk about Security?

52. What are the major Business Cost Optimization project milestones requiring communications or providing communications opportunities?

1.3 Stakeholder Analysis Matrix: Business Cost Optimization

53. Tactics: eg, surprise, major contracts?

54. Competitive advantages?

55. Where are mitigation costs factored in?

56. Organizational Applicability?

57. Benefit to whom?

58. Reputation, presence and reach?

59. Could any of your organizations weaknesses seriously threaten development?

60. Seasonality, weather effects?

61. Why do you care?

62. New technologies, services, ideas?

63. New USPs?

64. Effects on core activities, distraction?

65. Accreditations, qualifications, certifications?

66. Are the required specifications for products or services changing?

67. What makes a person a stakeholder?

68. What are the key services, contractual arrangements, or other relationships between stakeholder groups?

69. Who is most interested in information about the topic and/or has previously initiated interest?

70. Economy - home, abroad?

71. Industry or lifestyle trends?

72. Niche target markets?

2.0 Planning Process Group: Business Cost Optimization

73. What business situation is being addressed?

74. Will the products created live up to the necessary quality?

75. Is your organization showing technical capacity and leadership commitment to keep working with the Business Cost Optimization project and to repeat it?

76. Did the program design/ implementation strategy adequately address the planning stage necessary to set up structures, hire staff etc.?

77. Are the follow-up indicators relevant and do they meet the quality needed to measure the outputs and outcomes of the Business Cost Optimization project?

78. How does activity resource estimation affect activity duration estimation?

79. If you are late, will anybody notice?

80. In what way has the program contributed towards the issue culture and development included on the public agenda?

81. The Business Cost Optimization project charter is created in which Business Cost Optimization project management process group?

82. Does the program have follow-up mechanisms (to verify the quality of the products, punctuality of delivery, etc.) to measure progress in the achievement of the envisaged results?

83. Are you just doing busywork to pass the time?

84. Why do it Business Cost Optimization projects fail?

85. Is the Business Cost Optimization project supported by national and/or local organizations?

86. Are the necessary foundations in place to ensure the sustainability of the results of the Business Cost Optimization project?

87. To what extent are the visions and actions of the partners consistent or divergent with regard to the program?

88. How will you do it?

89. On which process should team members spend the most time?

90. What is the difference between the early schedule and late schedule?

91. Will you be replaced?

92. Contingency planning. if a risk event occurs, what will you do?

2.1 Project Management Plan: Business Cost Optimization

93. What is Business Cost Optimization project scope management?

94. What are the training needs?

95. Who is the Business Cost Optimization project Manager?

96. Are calculations and results of analyzes essentially correct?

97. What are the assumptions?

98. Are there non-structural buyout or relocation recommendations?

99. How can you best help your organization to develop consistent practices in Business Cost Optimization project management planning stages?

100. When is a Business Cost Optimization project management plan created?

101. What went wrong?

102. What data/reports/tools/etc. do program managers need?

103. Does the selected plan protect privacy?

104. Are the existing and future without-plan conditions reasonable and appropriate?

105. Does the implementation plan have an appropriate division of responsibilities?

106. Did the planning effort collaborate to develop solutions that integrate expertise, policies, programs, and Business Cost Optimization projects across entities?

107. Are there any Client staffing expectations?

108. Development trends and opportunities. What if the positive direction and vision of your organization causes expected trends to change?

109. Are there any scope changes proposed for a previously authorized Business Cost Optimization project?

110. What does management expect of PMs?

111. What happened during the process that you found interesting?

2.2 Scope Management Plan: Business Cost Optimization

112. How are you planning to maintain the scope baseline and how will you manage scope changes?

113. Do you document disagreements and work towards resolutions?

114. Does the business case include how the Business Cost Optimization project aligns with your organizations strategic goals & objectives?

115. Are procurement deliverables arriving on time and to specification?

116. Assess the expected stability of the scope of this Business Cost Optimization project how likely is it to change, how frequently, and by how much?

117. What threats might prevent you from getting there?

118. What problem is being solved by delivering this Business Cost Optimization project?

119. Staffing Requirements?

120. Do Business Cost Optimization project teams & team members report on status / activities / progress?

121. Organizational unit (e.g., department, team, or person) who will accept responsibility for satisfactory

completion of the item?

122. What do you need to do to accomplish the goal or goals?

123. Are vendor contract reports, reviews and visits conducted periodically?

124. Are mitigation strategies identified?

125. Have you identified possible roadblocks?

126. Is there a Steering Committee in place?

127. What are the risks that could significantly affect the communication on the Business Cost Optimization project?

128. Do you have funding for Business Cost Optimization project and product development, implementation and on-going support?

129. Is it possible to track all classes of Business Cost Optimization project work (e.g. scheduled, un-scheduled, defect repair, etc.)?

130. Is the schedule updated on a periodic basis?

2.3 Requirements Management Plan: Business Cost Optimization

131. Will you perform a Requirements Risk assessment and develop a plan to deal with risks?

132. How will you develop the schedule of requirements activities?

133. Will you have access to stakeholders when you need them?

134. How will requirements be managed?

135. Is any organizational data being used or stored?

136. Who will initially review the Business Cost Optimization project work or products to ensure it meets the applicable acceptance criteria?

137. Which hardware or software, related to, or as outcome of the Business Cost Optimization project is new to your organization?

138. Who is responsible for quantifying the Business Cost Optimization project requirements?

139. What are you trying to do?

140. How knowledgeable is the primary Stakeholder(s) in the proposed application area?

141. Define the help desk model. who will take full

responsibility?

142. What is a problem?

143. Did you provide clear and concise specifications?

144. Have stakeholders been instructed in the Change Control process?

145. Do you really need to write this document at all?

146. Is the user satisfied?

147. Is there formal agreement on who has authority to request a change in requirements?

148. Controlling Business Cost Optimization project requirements involves monitoring the status of the Business Cost Optimization project requirements and managing changes to the requirements. Who is responsible for monitoring and tracking the Business Cost Optimization project requirements?

149. How often will the reporting occur?

150. Did you use declarative statements?

2.4 Requirements Documentation: Business Cost Optimization

151. What if the system wasn t implemented?

152. Where do system and software requirements come from, what are sources?

153. Are all functions required by the customer included?

154. What marketing channels do you want to use: e-mail, letter or sms?

155. How does the proposed Business Cost Optimization project contribute to the overall objectives of your organization?

156. What are the acceptance criteria?

157. Can you check system requirements?

158. How do you get the user to tell you what they want?

159. How to document system requirements?

160. Do your constraints stand?

161. How do you know when a Requirement is accurate enough?

162. How much testing do you need to do to prove

that your system is safe?

163. What kind of entity is a problem ?

164. What are the potential disadvantages/
advantages?

165. How will requirements be documented and who
signs off on them?

166. Do technical resources exist?

167. Verifiability. can the requirements be checked?

168. What is your Elevator Speech?

169. Is the origin of the requirement clearly stated?

170. Who is involved?

2.5 Requirements Traceability Matrix: Business Cost Optimization

171. Describe the process for approving requirements so they can be added to the traceability matrix and Business Cost Optimization project work can be performed. Will the Business Cost Optimization project requirements become approved in writing?

172. What percentage of Business Cost Optimization projects are producing traceability matrices between requirements and other work products?

173. How small is small enough?

174. Is there a requirements traceability process in place?

175. Do you have a clear understanding of all subcontracts in place?

176. How will it affect the stakeholders personally in career?

177. Will you use a Requirements Traceability Matrix?

178. Why do you manage scope?

179. Why use a WBS?

180. What is the WBS?

181. How do you manage scope?

182. What are the chronologies, contingencies, consequences, criteria?

2.6 Project Scope Statement: Business Cost Optimization

183. Have the configuration management functions been assigned?

184. Any new risks introduced or old risks impacted. Are there issues that could affect the existing requirements for the result, service, or product if the scope changes?

185. Are there issues that could affect the existing requirements for the result, service, or product if the scope changes?

186. If you were to write a list of what should not be included in the scope statement, what are the things that you would recommend be described as out-of-scope?

187. Is the plan under configuration management?

188. Write a brief purpose statement for this Business Cost Optimization project. Include a business justification statement. What is the product of this Business Cost Optimization project?

189. Once its defined, what is the stability of the Business Cost Optimization project scope?

190. Are there backup strategies for key members of the Business Cost Optimization project?

191. Where and how does the team fit within your organization structure?

192. Does the scope statement still need some clarity?

193. Business Cost Optimization project lead, team lead, solution architect?

194. Identify how your team and you will create the Business Cost Optimization project scope statement and the work breakdown structure (WBS). Document how you will create the Business Cost Optimization project scope statement and WBS, and make sure you answer the following questions: In defining Business Cost Optimization project scope and the WBS, will you and your Business Cost Optimization project team be using methods defined by your organization, methods defined by the Business Cost Optimization project management office (PMO), or other methods?

195. Is this process communicated to the customer and team members?

196. Will this process be communicated to the customer and Business Cost Optimization project team?

197. Is your organization structure appropriate for the Business Cost Optimization projects size and complexity?

198. What is the product of this Business Cost Optimization project?

199. Did your Business Cost Optimization project ask for this?

200. If the scope changes, what will the impact be to your Business Cost Optimization project in terms of duration, cost, quality, or any other important areas of the Business Cost Optimization project?

201. Will the Business Cost Optimization project risks be managed according to the Business Cost Optimization projects risk management process?

202. What are the possible consequences should a risk come to occur?

2.7 Assumption and Constraint Log: Business Cost Optimization

203. Is there adequate stakeholder participation for the vetting of requirements definition, changes and management?

204. Is this process still needed?

205. What to do at recovery?

206. Security analysis has access to information that is sanitized?

207. Are there processes defining how software will be developed including development methods, overall timeline for development, software product standards, and traceability?

208. Have Business Cost Optimization project management standards and procedures been established and documented?

209. Has the approach and development strategy of the Business Cost Optimization project been defined, documented and accepted by the appropriate stakeholders?

210. Are there ways to reduce the time it takes to get something approved?

211. How do you design an auditing system?

212. Was the document/deliverable developed per the appropriate or required standards (for example, Institute of Electrical and Electronics Engineers standards)?

213. What do you audit?

214. What strengths do you have?

215. If appropriate, is the deliverable content consistent with current Business Cost Optimization project documents and in compliance with the Document Management Plan?

216. Does the system design reflect the requirements?

217. Have adequate resources been provided by management to ensure Business Cost Optimization project success?

218. What other teams / processes would be impacted by changes to the current process, and how?

219. What weaknesses do you have?

220. Does the document/deliverable meet all requirements (for example, statement of work) specific to this deliverable?

221. Can you perform this task or activity in a more effective manner?

222. Are there nonconformance issues?

2.8 Work Breakdown Structure: Business Cost Optimization

223. Do you need another level?

224. When does it have to be done?

225. How will you and your Business Cost Optimization project team define the Business Cost Optimization projects scope and work breakdown structure?

226. What is the probability that the Business Cost Optimization project duration will exceed xx weeks?

227. What is the probability of completing the Business Cost Optimization project in less that xx days?

228. How many levels?

229. What has to be done?

230. When do you stop?

231. How big is a work-package?

232. Where does it take place?

233. Why would you develop a Work Breakdown Structure?

234. How much detail?

235. Is it a change in scope?

236. Can you make it?

237. Who has to do it?

238. Why is it useful?

239. Is the work breakdown structure (wbs) defined and is the scope of the Business Cost Optimization project clear with assigned deliverable owners?

2.9 WBS Dictionary: Business Cost Optimization

240. Do work packages consist of discrete tasks which are adequately described?

241. Are indirect costs charged to the appropriate indirect pools and incurring organization?

242. Are current budgets resulting from changes to the authorized work and/or internal replanning, reconcilable to original budgets for specified reporting items?

243. Are the variances between budgeted and actual indirect costs identified and analyzed at the level of assigned responsibility for control (indirect pool, department, etc.)?

244. What are you counting on?

245. Is work progressively subdivided into detailed work packages as requirements are defined?

246. Are Business Cost Optimization projected overhead costs in each pool and the associated direct costs used as the basis for establishing interim rates for allocating overhead to contracts?

247. Are all affected work authorizations, budgeting, and scheduling documents amended to properly reflect the effects of authorized changes?

248. The wbs is developed as part of a joint planning session. and how do you know that youhave done this right?

249. Does the contractors system provide for the determination of cost variances attributable to the excess usage of material?

250. Are all authorized tasks assigned to identified organizational elements?

251. Are data elements summarized through the functional organizational structure for progressively higher levels of management?

252. Where engineering standards or other internal work measurement systems are used, is there a formal relationship between corresponding values and work package budgets?

253. Are overhead cost budgets (or Business Cost Optimization projections) established on a facility-wide basis at least annually for the life of the contract?

254. Are the wbs and organizational levels for application of the Business Cost Optimization projected overhead costs identified?

255. Does the contractor require sufficient detailed planning of control accounts to constrain the application of budget initially allocated for future effort to current effort?

256. Are control accounts opened and closed based on the start and completion of work contained therein?

257. Is cost and schedule performance measurement done in a consistent, systematic manner?

2.10 Schedule Management Plan: Business Cost Optimization

258. Are metrics used to evaluate and manage Vendors?

259. Is pert / critical path or equivalent methodology being used?

260. Is the schedule feasible and at what cost?

261. Were Business Cost Optimization project team members involved in detailed estimating and scheduling?

262. Is there an onboarding process in place?

263. Have activity relationships and interdependencies within tasks been adequately identified?

264. Are there any activities or deliverables being added or gold-plated that could be dropped or scaled back without falling short of the original requirement?

265. Which status reports are received per the Business Cost Optimization project Plan?

266. Does the detailed work plan match the complexity of tasks with the capabilities of personnel?

267. Are the primary and secondary schedule tools defined?

268. Is the schedule vertically and horizontally traceable?

269. Is the ims used by all levels of management for Business Cost Optimization project implementation and control?

270. Is a payment system in place with proper reviews and approvals?

271. Are tasks tracked by hours?

272. Are there checklists created to determine if all quality processes are followed?

273. Are the Business Cost Optimization project team members located locally to the users/stakeholders?

274. Does the Business Cost Optimization project have a formal Business Cost Optimization project Charter?

275. Pareto diagrams, statistical sampling, flow charting or trend analysis used quality monitoring?

276. Do Business Cost Optimization project teams & team members report on status / activities / progress?

277. Alignment to strategic goals & objectives?

2.11 Activity List: Business Cost Optimization

278. How much slack is available in the Business Cost Optimization project?

279. For other activities, how much delay can be tolerated?

280. How do you determine the late start (LS) for each activity?

281. Is infrastructure setup part of your Business Cost Optimization project?

282. When do the individual activities need to start and finish?

283. What are the critical bottleneck activities?

284. Should you include sub-activities?

285. How detailed should a Business Cost Optimization project get?

286. What is the probability the Business Cost Optimization project can be completed in xx weeks?

287. Is there anything planned that does not need to be here?

288. In what sequence?

289. What went right?

290. How will it be performed?

291. Can you determine the activity that must finish, before this activity can start?

292. What did not go as well?

293. How should ongoing costs be monitored to try to keep the Business Cost Optimization project within budget?

294. How difficult will it be to do specific activities on this Business Cost Optimization project?

295. What will be performed?

2.12 Activity Attributes: Business Cost Optimization

296. Are the required resources available or need to be acquired?

297. What activity do you think you should spend the most time on?

298. Resources to accomplish the work?

299. Time for overtime?

300. What is missing?

301. Activity: fair or not fair?

302. Do you feel very comfortable with your prediction?

303. Activity: what is In the Bag?

304. Can more resources be added?

305. How difficult will it be to complete specific activities on this Business Cost Optimization project?

306. How difficult will it be to do specific activities on this Business Cost Optimization project?

307. What is your organizations history in doing similar activities?

308. Where else does it apply?

309. Activity: what is Missing?

310. What conclusions/generalizations can you draw from this?

311. Have you identified the Activity Leveling Priority code value on each activity?

312. Has management defined a definite timeframe for the turnaround or Business Cost Optimization project window?

313. Resource is assigned to?

314. Have constraints been applied to the start and finish milestones for the phases?

2.13 Milestone List: Business Cost Optimization

315. What is the market for your technology, product or service?

316. Describe the concept of the technology, product or service that will be or has been developed. How will it be used?

317. How will you get the word out to customers?

318. Who will manage the Business Cost Optimization project on a day-to-day basis?

319. Gaps in capabilities?

320. Milestone pages should display the UserID of the person who added the milestone. Does a report or query exist that provides this audit information?

321. Vital contracts and partners?

322. Loss of key staff?

323. How will the milestone be verified?

324. What are your competitors vulnerabilities?

325. When will the Business Cost Optimization project be complete?

326. Describe the industry you are in and the market

growth opportunities. What is the market for your technology, product or service?

327. What would happen if a delivery of material was one week late?

328. Information and research?

329. How soon can the activity start?

330. How difficult will it be to do specific activities on this Business Cost Optimization project?

331. Own known vulnerabilities?

332. How late can the activity start?

2.14 Network Diagram: Business Cost Optimization

333. What to do and When?

334. What is the completion time?

335. What activities must occur simultaneously with this activity?

336. Which type of network diagram allows you to depict four types of dependencies?

337. Will crashing x weeks return more in benefits than it costs?

338. Are you on time?

339. What can be done concurrently?

340. Are the gantt chart and/or network diagram updated periodically and used to assess the overall Business Cost Optimization project timetable?

341. Can you calculate the confidence level?

342. What job or jobs precede it?

343. What activities must follow this activity?

344. If x is long, what would be the completion time if you break x into two parallel parts of y weeks and z weeks?

345. What controls the start and finish of a job?

346. What is the probability of completing the Business Cost Optimization project in less that xx days?

347. Review the logical flow of the network diagram. Take a look at which activities you have first and then sequence the activities. Do they make sense?

348. Where do schedules come from?

349. What job or jobs could run concurrently?

350. What is the lowest cost to complete this Business Cost Optimization project in xx weeks?

351. Planning: who, how long, what to do?

352. If the Business Cost Optimization project network diagram cannot change and you have extra personnel resources, what is the BEST thing to do?

2.15 Activity Resource Requirements: Business Cost Optimization

353. When does monitoring begin?

354. Other support in specific areas?

355. Anything else?

356. How many signatures do you require on a check and does this match what is in your policy and procedures?

357. What is the Work Plan Standard?

358. What are constraints that you might find during the Human Resource Planning process?

359. Are there unresolved issues that need to be addressed?

360. How do you handle petty cash?

361. Do you use tools like decomposition and rolling-wave planning to produce the activity list and other outputs?

362. Why do you do that?

363. Which logical relationship does the PDM use most often?

364. How do you manage time?

2.16 Resource Breakdown Structure: Business Cost Optimization

365. Why time management?

366. How difficult will it be to do specific activities on this Business Cost Optimization project?

367. What is the purpose of assigning and documenting responsibility?

368. What is the number one predictor of a groups productivity?

369. Which resource planning tool provides information on resource responsibility and accountability?

370. Goals for the Business Cost Optimization project. What is each stakeholders desired outcome for the Business Cost Optimization project?

371. Who is allowed to perform which functions?

372. What can you do to improve productivity?

373. Is predictive resource analysis being done?

374. Who will use the system?

375. How should the information be delivered?

376. The list could probably go on, but, the thing that

you would most like to know is, How long & How much?

377. What defines a successful Business Cost Optimization project?

378. Changes based on input from stakeholders?

379. Who delivers the information?

380. How can this help you with team building?

2.17 Activity Duration Estimates: Business Cost Optimization

381. Are expert judgment and historical information utilized to estimate activity duration?

382. Are the causes of all variances identified?

383. Are contractor costs, schedule and technical performance monitored throughout the Business Cost Optimization project?

384. What is earned value?

385. What are the Business Cost Optimization project management deliverables of each process group?

386. (Cpi), and schedule performance index (spi) for the Business Cost Optimization project?

387. Are changes to the scope managed according to defined procedures?

388. Briefly summarize the work done by Maslow, Herzberg, McClellan, McGregor, Ouchi, Thamhain and Wilemon, and Covey. How do theories relate to Business Cost Optimization project management?

389. Do scope statements include the Business Cost Optimization project objectives and expected deliverables?

390. Are Business Cost Optimization project activities

decomposed into manageable components to ensure expected management control?

391. How could you use each technique in your organization?

392. What are the largest companies that provide information technology outsourcing services?

393. Will the new application be developed using existing hardware, software, and networks?

394. What is the difference between using brainstorming and the Delphi technique for risk identification?

395. Is the work performed reviewed against contractual objectives?

396. List five reasons why organizations outsource. Why is there a growing trend in outsourcing, especially in the government?

397. Are Business Cost Optimization project costs tracked in the general ledger?

398. Which is correct?

2.18 Duration Estimating Worksheet: Business Cost Optimization

399. Why estimate costs?

400. Done before proceeding with this activity or what can be done concurrently?

401. How should ongoing costs be monitored to try to keep the Business Cost Optimization project within budget?

402. What utility impacts are there?

403. Will the Business Cost Optimization project collaborate with the local community and leverage resources?

404. Small or large Business Cost Optimization project?

405. Do any colleagues have experience with your organization and/or RFPs?

406. What is an Average Business Cost Optimization project?

407. Is the Business Cost Optimization project responsive to community need?

408. How can the Business Cost Optimization project be displayed graphically to better visualize the activities?

409. When does your organization expect to be able to complete it?

410. Value pocket identification & quantification what are value pockets?

411. What info is needed?

412. Is this operation cost effective?

413. Does the Business Cost Optimization project provide innovative ways for stakeholders to overcome obstacles or deliver better outcomes?

414. When, then?

415. What work will be included in the Business Cost Optimization project?

2.19 Project Schedule: Business Cost Optimization

416. Schedule/cost recovery?

417. How closely did the initial Business Cost Optimization project Schedule compare with the actual schedule?

418. How does a Business Cost Optimization project get to be a year late ?

419. To what degree is do you feel the entire team was committed to the Business Cost Optimization project schedule?

420. What is risk?

421. What is risk management?

422. Is there a Schedule Management Plan that establishes the criteria and activities for developing, monitoring and controlling the Business Cost Optimization project schedule?

423. How can slack be negative?

424. How do you manage Business Cost Optimization project Risk?

425. Activity charts and bar charts are graphical representations of a Business Cost Optimization project schedule ...how do they differ?

426. Are procedures defined by which the Business Cost Optimization project schedule may be changed?

427. Is Business Cost Optimization project work proceeding in accordance with the original Business Cost Optimization project schedule?

428. Are you working on the right risks?

429. How detailed should a Business Cost Optimization project get?

430. Did the Business Cost Optimization project come in on schedule?

431. Master Business Cost Optimization project schedule?

2.20 Cost Management Plan: Business Cost Optimization

432. Are vendor invoices audited for accuracy before payment?

433. Are Business Cost Optimization project team members committed fulltime?

434. Are meeting minutes captured and sent out after the meeting?

435. Have all unresolved risks been documented?

436. Are Business Cost Optimization project team members involved in detailed estimating and scheduling?

437. Has a structured approach been used to break work effort into manageable components (WBS)?

438. Business Cost Optimization project definition & scope?

439. Is the steering committee active in Business Cost Optimization project oversight?

440. Has a resource management plan been created?

441. What would you do differently what did not work?

442. Do Business Cost Optimization project managers

participating in the Business Cost Optimization project know the Business Cost Optimization projects true status first hand?

443. Is quality monitored from the perspective of the customers needs and expectations?

444. Vac -variance at completion, how much over/ under budget do you expect to be?

445. Are all payments made according to the contract(s)?

446. Are Business Cost Optimization project contact logs kept up to date?

447. Are changes in deliverable commitments agreed to by all affected groups & individuals?

448. Is there general agreement & acceptance of the current status and progress of the Business Cost Optimization project?

449. Is there a formal set of procedures supporting Stakeholder Management?

450. Scope of work – What is the scope of work for each of the planned contracts?

2.21 Activity Cost Estimates: Business Cost Optimization

451. How and when do you enter into Business Cost Optimization project Procurement Management?

452. Can you change your activities?

453. Based on your Business Cost Optimization project communication management plan, what worked well?

454. Are cost subtotals needed?

455. Where can you get activity reports?

456. How do you do activity recasts?

457. Was it performed on time?

458. How quickly can the task be done with the skills available?

459. How do you allocate indirect costs to activities?

460. Were escalated issues resolved promptly?

461. Would you hire them again?

462. What are the audit requirements?

463. How Award?

464. What areas were overlooked on this Business Cost Optimization project?

465. What happens if you cannot produce the documentation for the single audit?

466. What do you want to know about the stay to know if costs were inappropriately high or low?

467. What defines a successful Business Cost Optimization project?

468. What is Business Cost Optimization project cost management?

469. Will you need to provide essential services information about activities?

2.22 Cost Estimating Worksheet: Business Cost Optimization

470. Ask: are others positioned to know, are others credible, and will others cooperate?

471. Identify the timeframe necessary to monitor progress and collect data to determine how the selected measure has changed?

472. Who is best positioned to know and assist in identifying corresponding factors?

473. Is the Business Cost Optimization project responsive to community need?

474. What is the purpose of estimating?

475. How will the results be shared and to whom?

476. What can be included?

477. What costs are to be estimated?

478. Is it feasible to establish a control group arrangement?

479. What additional Business Cost Optimization project(s) could be initiated as a result of this Business Cost Optimization project?

480. What will others want?

481. What happens to any remaining funds not used?

482. Will the Business Cost Optimization project collaborate with the local community and leverage resources?

483. Can a trend be established from historical performance data on the selected measure and are the criteria for using trend analysis or forecasting methods met?

484. Does the Business Cost Optimization project provide innovative ways for stakeholders to overcome obstacles or deliver better outcomes?

485. What is the estimated labor cost today based upon this information?

2.23 Cost Baseline: Business Cost Optimization

486. How long are you willing to wait before you find out were late?

487. Has the documentation relating to operation and maintenance of the product(s) or service(s) been delivered to, and accepted by, operations management?

488. Who will use corresponding metrics ?

489. Has the Business Cost Optimization projected annual cost to operate and maintain the product(s) or service(s) been approved and funded?

490. Is request in line with priorities?

491. What is your organizations history in doing similar tasks?

492. Where do changes come from?

493. Have all approved changes to the schedule baseline been identified and impact on the Business Cost Optimization project documented?

494. Has the appropriate access to relevant data and analysis capability been granted?

495. Is there anything unique in this Business Cost Optimization projects scope statement that will affect

resources?

496. Is the requested change request a result of changes in other Business Cost Optimization project(s)?

497. Does the suggested change request seem to represent a necessary enhancement to the product?

498. Impact to environment?

499. Does the suggested change request represent a desired enhancement to the products functionality?

500. For what purpose ?

501. Are you asking management for something as a result of this update?

502. What do you want to measure ?

503. Does a process exist for establishing a cost baseline to measure Business Cost Optimization project performance?

2.24 Quality Management Plan: Business Cost Optimization

504. Are there standards for code development?

505. What changes can you make that will result in improvement?

506. How does your organization decide what to measure?

507. Is the steering committee active in Business Cost Optimization project oversight?

508. Are there procedures in place to effectively manage interdependencies with other Business Cost Optimization projects / systems?

509. Is it necessary?

510. How is staff trained on the recording of field notes?

511. What are your results for key measures/indicators of accomplishment of organizational strategy?

512. What is the audience for the data?

513. Diagrams and tables to account for complex concepts and increase overall readability?

514. How are training records kept?

515. With the five whys method, the team considers why the issue being explored occurred. do others then take that initial answer and ask why?

516. Who is responsible?

517. How is staff trained in procedures?

518. How does your organization address regulatory, legal, and ethical compliance?

519. No superfluous information or marketing narrative?

520. Is this a Requirement?

521. What is quality and how will you ensure it?

522. How do you prioritize?

523. You know what your customers expectations are regarding this process?

2.25 Quality Metrics: Business Cost Optimization

524. Can you correlate your quality metrics to profitability?

525. Was review conducted per standard protocols?

526. Is the reporting frequency appropriate?

527. What is the timeline to meet your goal?

528. What can manufacturing professionals do to ensure quality is seen as an integral part of the entire product lifecycle?

529. What metrics are important and most beneficial to measure?

530. There are many reasons to shore up quality-related metrics, and what metrics are important?

531. Subjective quality component: customer satisfaction, how do you measure it?

532. Are documents on hand to provide explanations of privacy and confidentiality?

533. Has it met internal or external standards?

534. Do you stratify metrics by product or site?

535. What about still open problems?

536. Were number of defects identified?

537. How do you calculate corresponding metrics?

538. What if the biggest risk to your business were the already stated people who do not complain?

539. Was the overall quality better or worse than previous products?

540. What level of statistical confidence do you use?

541. What group is empowered to define quality requirements?

542. Is material complete (and does it meet the standards)?

543. What are your organizations expectations for its quality Business Cost Optimization project?

2.26 Process Improvement Plan: Business Cost Optimization

544. Why quality management?

545. What is the test-cycle concept?

546. Has a process guide to collect the data been developed?

547. Have storage and access mechanisms and procedures been determined?

548. Have the frequency of collection and the points in the process where measurements will be made been determined?

549. Has the time line required to move measurement results from the points of collection to databases or users been established?

550. What personnel are the sponsors for that initiative?

551. Are you making progress on the improvement framework?

552. Where are you now?

553. What personnel are the change agents for your initiative?

554. Have the supporting tools been developed or

acquired?

555. The motive is determined by asking, Why do you want to achieve this goal?

556. What lessons have you learned so far?

557. Why do you want to achieve the goal?

558. Does your process ensure quality?

559. Management commitment at all levels?

560. What personnel are the champions for the initiative?

561. To elicit goal statements, do you ask a question such as, What do you want to achieve?

562. Are you making progress on the goals?

2.27 Responsibility Assignment Matrix: Business Cost Optimization

563. Are too many reports done in writing instead of verbally?

564. Does the contractor use objective results, design reviews and tests to trace schedule performance?

565. Does the contractors system provide unit or lot costs when applicable?

566. Authorization to proceed with all authorized work?

567. Are significant decision points, constraints, and interfaces identified as key milestones?

568. Are the actual costs used for variance analysis reconcilable with data from the accounting system?

569. Does the accounting system provide a basis for auditing records of direct costs chargeable to the contract?

570. Are estimates of costs at completion generated in a rational, consistent manner?

571. Budgeted cost for work performed?

572. The staff characteristics – is the group or the person capable to work together as a team?

573. Not any rs, as, or cs: if an identified role is only informed, should others be eliminated from the matrix?

574. Do others have the time to dedicate to your Business Cost Optimization project?

575. Are data elements reconcilable between internal summary reports and reports forwarded to stakeholders?

576. How cost benefit analysis?

577. What expertise is available in your department?

578. Does the contractor use objective results, design reviews, and tests to trace schedule?

579. How do you assist them to be as productive as possible?

580. Major functional areas of contract effort?

2.28 Roles and Responsibilities: Business Cost Optimization

581. Accountabilities: what are the roles and responsibilities of individual team members?

582. What should you do now to prepare for your career 5+ years from now?

583. How is your work-life balance?

584. What specific behaviors did you observe?

585. What should you highlight for improvement?

586. Are governance roles and responsibilities documented?

587. Who: who is involved?

588. What areas would you highlight for changes or improvements?

589. What should you do now to ensure that you are meeting all expectations of your current position?

590. Are the quality assurance functions and related roles and responsibilities clearly defined?

591. How well did the Business Cost Optimization project Team understand the expectations of specific roles and responsibilities?

592. What should you do now to prepare yourself for a promotion, increased responsibilities or a different job?

593. To decide whether to use a quality measurement, ask how will you know when it is achieved?

594. What is working well?

595. Who is responsible for each task?

596. Are your policies supportive of a culture of quality data?

597. Does the team have access to and ability to use data analysis tools?

598. What expectations were NOT met?

2.29 Human Resource Management Plan: Business Cost Optimization

599. Have the key functions and capabilities been defined and assigned to each release or iteration?

600. Is there a requirements change management processes in place?

601. Has a quality assurance plan been developed for the Business Cost Optimization project?

602. How do you determine what key skills and talents are needed to meet the objectives. Is your organization primarily focused on a specific industry?

603. Is there an issues management plan in place?

604. Have external dependencies been captured in the schedule?

605. How are you going to ensure that you have a well motivated workforce?

606. Is there a Quality Management Plan?

607. Are Business Cost Optimization project team members committed fulltime?

608. Are all resource assumptions documented?

609. Are staff skills known and available for each task?

610. Is there an approved case?

611. Is there an on-going process in place to monitor Business Cost Optimization project risks?

612. Were Business Cost Optimization project team members involved in detailed estimating and scheduling?

613. Are adequate resources provided for the quality assurance function?

614. Are Business Cost Optimization project team roles and responsibilities identified and documented?

615. Have all necessary approvals been obtained?

2.30 Communications Management Plan: Business Cost Optimization

616. Where do team members get information?

617. Who did you turn to if you had questions?

618. How is this initiative related to other portfolios, programs, or Business Cost Optimization projects?

619. Do you have members of your team responsible for certain stakeholders?

620. How do you manage communications?

621. How did the term stakeholder originate?

622. Are the stakeholders getting the information others need, are others consulted, are concerns addressed?

623. Do you ask; can you recommend others for you to talk with about this initiative?

624. Who will use or be affected by the result of a Business Cost Optimization project?

625. What approaches do you use?

626. Who is involved as you identify stakeholders?

627. Why do you manage communications?

628. What are the interrelationships?

629. How much time does it take to do it?

630. Are others needed?

631. What is the political influence?

632. Who to share with?

633. Are there potential barriers between the team and the stakeholder?

2.31 Risk Management Plan: Business Cost Optimization

634. Are there new risks that mitigation strategies might introduce?

635. Is the necessary data being captured and is it complete and accurate?

636. Why might it be late?

637. Is the customer willing to commit significant time to the requirements gathering process?

638. What is the impact to the Business Cost Optimization project if the item is not resolved in a timely fashion?

639. Why do you want risk management?

640. Was an original risk assessment/risk management plan completed?

641. How can you fix it?

642. Why is product liability a serious issue?

643. What is the probability the risk avoidance strategy will be successful?

644. Is the customer willing to participate in reviews?

645. How quickly does each item need to be resolved?

646. Are people attending meetings and doing work?

647. What things might go wrong?

648. Are the best people available?

649. Degree of confidence in estimated size estimate?

650. User involvement: do you have the right users?

651. Mitigation -how can you avoid the risk?

652. Are the reports useful and easy to read?

653. What are the cost, schedule and resource impacts of avoiding the risk?

2.32 Risk Register: Business Cost Optimization

654. When would you develop a risk register?

655. Does the evidence highlight any areas to advance opportunities or foster good relations. If yes what steps will be taken?

656. What could prevent you delivering on the strategic program objectives and what is being done to mitigate corresponding issues?

657. What is your current and future risk profile?

658. Who needs to know about this?

659. What are your key risks/show istoppers and what is being done to manage them?

660. Can the likelihood and impact of failing to achieve corresponding recommendations and action plans be assessed?

661. What is a Risk?

662. What are the assumptions and current status that support the assessment of the risk?

663. What risks might negatively or positively affect achieving the Business Cost Optimization project objectives?

664. What further options might be available for responding to the risk?

665. People risk -are people with appropriate skills available to help complete the Business Cost Optimization project?

666. What is the reason for current performance gaps and do the risks and opportunities identified previously account for this?

667. Are implemented controls working as others should?

668. What evidence do you have to justify the likelihood score of the risk (audit, incident report, claim, complaints, inspection, internal review)?

669. How are risks graded?

670. How often will the Risk Management Plan and Risk Register be formally reviewed, and by whom?

671. What are you going to do to limit the Business Cost Optimization projects risk exposure due to the identified risks?

672. What may happen or not go according to plan?

2.33 Probability and Impact Assessment: Business Cost Optimization

673. Are the risk data timely and relevant?

674. Is there additional information that would make you more confident about your analysis?

675. Are trained personnel, including supervisors and Business Cost Optimization project managers, available to handle such a large Business Cost Optimization project?

676. What can you do about it?

677. Risk urgency assessment -which of your risks could occur soon, or require a longer planning time?

678. Which functions, departments, and activities of your organization are going to be affected?

679. Can the Business Cost Optimization project proceed without assuming the risk?

680. Does the Business Cost Optimization project team have experience with the technology to be implemented?

681. What should be the external organizations responsibility vis-à-vis total stake in the Business Cost Optimization project?

682. What are the industrial relations prevailing in your organization?

683. How risk averse are you?

684. What would be the effect of slippage?

685. How is the Business Cost Optimization project going to be managed?

686. What kind of preparation would be required to do this?

687. Are tool mentors available?

688. Are there any Business Cost Optimization projects similar to this one in existence?

689. What are the current requirements of the customer?

690. Can you avoid altogether some things that might go wrong?

691. My Business Cost Optimization project leader has suddenly left your organization, what do you do?

692. How well is the risk understood?

2.34 Probability and Impact Matrix: Business Cost Optimization

693. Do the people have the right combinations of skills?

694. Should the risk be taken at all?

695. Do others match with the clients requirement?

696. Have you worked with the customer in the past?

697. Non-valid or incredible information?

698. Sensitivity analysis -which risks will have the most impact on the Business Cost Optimization project?

699. Are the risk data complete?

700. Are tools for analysis and design available?

701. What are its business ethics?

702. What will be the likely political situation during the life of the Business Cost Optimization project?

703. What should be done with risks on the watch list?

704. Is Business Cost Optimization project scope stable?

705. What will be cost of redeployment of the

personnel?

706. What risks were tracked?

707. Is there any sign of biased ranking?

708. Do you know the order of planning yet?

709. Economic to take on the Business Cost Optimization project?

710. How can you understand and diagnose risks and identify sources?

711. How is the risk management process used in practice?

712. Is the process supported by tools?

2.35 Risk Data Sheet: Business Cost Optimization

713. What is the environment within which you operate (social trends, economic, community values, broad based participation, national directions etc.)?

714. What can happen?

715. What do people affected think about the need for, and practicality of preventive measures?

716. How can hazards be reduced?

717. Are new hazards created?

718. What were the Causes that contributed?

719. Has the most cost-effective solution been chosen?

720. What are the main opportunities available to you that you should grab while you can?

721. How do you handle product safely?

722. Has a sensitivity analysis been carried out?

723. How can it happen?

724. What can you do?

725. Is the data sufficiently specified in terms of the

type of failure being analyzed, and its frequency or probability?

726. What are you trying to achieve (Objectives)?

727. If it happens, what are the consequences?

728. How reliable is the data source?

729. Who has a vested interest in how you perform as your organization (our stakeholders)?

730. Potential for recurrence?

2.36 Procurement Management Plan: Business Cost Optimization

731. Was the scope definition used in task sequencing?

732. Are cause and effect determined for risks when others occur?

733. Has the schedule been baselined?

734. If independent estimates will be needed as evaluation criteria, who will prepare them and when?

735. What types of contracts will be used?

736. How long will it take for the purchase cost to be the same as the lease cost?

737. Are the Business Cost Optimization project team members located locally to the users/stakeholders?

738. Are meeting minutes captured and sent out after meetings?

739. Are the payment terms being followed?

740. Are decisions made in a timely manner?

741. Has a quality assurance plan been developed for the Business Cost Optimization project?

742. How will multiple providers be managed?

743. Business Cost Optimization project Objectives?

744. Are trade-offs between accepting the risk and mitigating the risk identified?

745. Have key stakeholders been identified?

746. Are internal Business Cost Optimization project status meetings held at reasonable intervals?

747. Are post milestone Business Cost Optimization project reviews (PMPR) conducted with your organization at least once a year?

2.37 Source Selection Criteria: Business Cost Optimization

748. Is the contracting office likely to receive more purchase requests for this item or service during the coming year?

749. How do you manage procurement?

750. What information may not be provided?

751. In which phase of the acquisition process cycle does source qualifications reside?

752. When is it appropriate to issue a DRFP?

753. How can solicitation Schedules be improved to yield more effective price competition?

754. Who is on the Source Selection Advisory Committee?

755. How much past performance information should be requested?

756. Do you have designated specific forms or worksheets?

757. Are resultant proposal revisions allowed?

758. How can business terms and conditions be improved to yield more effective price competition?

759. What should be the contracting officers strategy?

760. How should oral presentations be prepared for?

761. What source selection software is your team using?

762. How much weight should be placed on past performance information?

763. Are responses to considerations adequate?

764. What common questions or problems are associated with debriefings?

765. Are types/quantities of material, facilities appropriate?

766. Are evaluators ready to begin this task?

767. What does an evaluation address and what does a sample resemble?

2.38 Stakeholder Management Plan: Business Cost Optimization

768. Have all team members been part of identifying risks?

769. What is meant by managing the triple constraint?

770. Are internal Business Cost Optimization project status meetings held at reasonable intervals?

771. Has the budget been baselined?

772. Are the appropriate IT resources adequate to meet planned commitments?

773. Are post milestone Business Cost Optimization project reviews (PMPR) conducted with your organization at least once a year?

774. At what point will the Business Cost Optimization project be closed and what will be done to formally close the Business Cost Optimization project?

775. Where will verification occur, and by whom?

776. Are the schedule estimates reasonable given the Business Cost Optimization project?

777. How are stakeholders chosen and what roles might they have on a Business Cost Optimization project?

778. Is Business Cost Optimization project status reviewed with the steering and executive teams at appropriate intervals?

779. Are decisions captured in a decisions log?

780. Is the amount of effort justified by the anticipated value of forming a new process?

781. Is the steering committee active in Business Cost Optimization project oversight?

782. Is staff trained on the software technologies that are being used on the Business Cost Optimization project?

783. Is documentation created for communication with the suppliers and vendors?

2.39 Change Management Plan: Business Cost Optimization

784. What prerequisite knowledge or training is required?

785. Will a different work structure focus people on what is important?

786. What risks may occur upfront, during implementation and after implementation?

787. What are the specific target groups / audience that will be impacted by this change?

788. What is the reason for the communication?

789. What is the most positive interpretation it can receive?

790. When does it make sense to customize?

791. What did the people around you say about it?

792. Where will the funds come from?

793. Have the business unit contacts been selected and notified?

794. Will the culture embrace or reject this change?

795. How do you know the requirements you documented are the right ones?

796. Have the approved procedures and policies been published?

797. Do you need a new organizational structure?

798. Why is it important?

799. What are the training strategies?

800. What roles within your organization are affected, and how?

801. Has the target training audience been identified and nominated?

802. What provokes organizational change?

3.0 Executing Process Group: Business Cost Optimization

803. What factors are contributing to progress or delay in the achievement of products and results?

804. Why do you need a good WBS to use Business Cost Optimization project management software?

805. Would you rate yourself as being risk-averse, risk-neutral, or risk-seeking?

806. If action is called for, what form should it take?

807. How can software assist in procuring goods and services?

808. What are the main processes included in Business Cost Optimization project quality management?

809. What is the critical path for this Business Cost Optimization project and how long is it?

810. What areas were overlooked on this Business Cost Optimization project?

811. Is the program supported by national and/or local organizations?

812. In what way has the program come up with innovative measures for problem-solving?

813. How will you avoid scope creep?

814. It under budget or over budget?

815. How does the job market and current state of the economy affect human resource management?

816. How does Business Cost Optimization project management relate to other disciplines?

817. How do you enter durations, link tasks, and view critical path information?

818. Does the Business Cost Optimization project team have the right skills?

819. Who are the Business Cost Optimization project stakeholders?

820. What are deliverables of your Business Cost Optimization project?

821. How well did the chosen processes produce the expected results?

822. How could you control progress of your Business Cost Optimization project?

3.1 Team Member Status Report: Business Cost Optimization

823. How can you make it practical?

824. Are the products of your organizations Business Cost Optimization projects meeting customers objectives?

825. How will resource planning be done?

826. What specific interest groups do you have in place?

827. Are your organizations Business Cost Optimization projects more successful over time?

828. Why is it to be done?

829. Does the product, good, or service already exist within your organization?

830. Will the staff do training or is that done by a third party?

831. Is there evidence that staff is taking a more professional approach toward management of your organizations Business Cost Optimization projects?

832. Do you have an Enterprise Business Cost Optimization project Management Office (EPMO)?

833. What is to be done?

834. Are the attitudes of staff regarding Business Cost Optimization project work improving?

835. When a teams productivity and success depend on collaboration and the efficient flow of information, what generally fails them?

836. Does every department have to have a Business Cost Optimization project Manager on staff?

837. How does this product, good, or service meet the needs of the Business Cost Optimization project and your organization as a whole?

838. How much risk is involved?

839. How it is to be done?

840. The problem with Reward & Recognition Programs is that the truly deserving people all too often get left out. How can you make it practical?

841. Does your organization have the means (staff, money, contract, etc.) to produce or to acquire the product, good, or service?

3.2 Change Request: Business Cost Optimization

842. Who is communicating the change?

843. How to get changes (code) out in a timely manner?

844. Who is included in the change control team?

845. Has a formal technical review been conducted to assess technical correctness?

846. Change request coordination ?

847. Will there be a change request form in use?

848. Are you implementing itil processes?

849. What type of changes does change control take into account?

850. Will all change requests and current status be logged?

851. Is it feasible to use requirements attributes as predictors of reliability?

852. What is a Change Request Form?

853. What is the relationship between requirements attributes and attributes like complexity and size?

854. For which areas does this operating procedure apply?

855. Can you answer what happened, who did it, when did it happen, and what else will be affected?

856. How can you ensure that changes have been made properly?

857. How do team members communicate with each other?

858. What needs to be communicated?

859. What can be filed?

860. Should a more thorough impact analysis be conducted?

3.3 Change Log: Business Cost Optimization

861. Is the change backward compatible without limitations?

862. When was the request approved?

863. Do the described changes impact on the integrity or security of the system?

864. Is the requested change request a result of changes in other Business Cost Optimization project(s)?

865. Is the change request within Business Cost Optimization project scope?

866. Is this a mandatory replacement?

867. Is the change request open, closed or pending?

868. How does this change affect the timeline of the schedule?

869. When was the request submitted?

870. Is the submitted change a new change or a modification of a previously approved change?

871. Who initiated the change request?

872. How does this relate to the standards developed

for specific business processes?

873. How does this change affect scope?

874. Will the Business Cost Optimization project fail if the change request is not executed?

3.4 Decision Log: Business Cost Optimization

875. Is your opponent open to a non-traditional workflow, or will it likely challenge anything you do?

876. Is everything working as expected?

877. What makes you different or better than others companies selling the same thing?

878. Behaviors; what are guidelines that the team has identified that will assist them with getting the most out of team meetings?

879. What are the cost implications?

880. Decision-making process; how will the team make decisions?

881. Linked to original objective?

882. Who will be given a copy of this document and where will it be kept?

883. How do you define success?

884. What alternatives/risks were considered?

885. Does anything need to be adjusted?

886. How does an increasing emphasis on cost containment influence the strategies and tactics

used?

887. How does the use a Decision Support System influence the strategies/tactics or costs?

888. Which variables make a critical difference?

889. How does provision of information, both in terms of content and presentation, influence acceptance of alternative strategies?

890. At what point in time does loss become unacceptable?

891. What is the average size of your matters in an applicable measurement?

892. How effective is maintaining the log at facilitating organizational learning?

893. It becomes critical to track and periodically revisit both operational effectiveness; Are you noticing all that you need to, and are you interpreting what you see effectively?

894. What is your overall strategy for quality control / quality assurance procedures?

3.5 Quality Audit: Business Cost Optimization

895. Are storage areas and reconditioning operations designed to prevent mix-ups and assure orderly handling of both the distressed and reconditioned devices?

896. How are you auditing your organizations compliance with regulations?

897. Are the policies and processes, as set out in the Quality Audit Manual, properly applied?

898. How does your organization know that its processes for managing severance are appropriately effective, constructive and fair?

899. What has changed/improved as a result of the review processes?

900. What is the collective experience of the team to be assigned to an audit?

901. Is the process of self review, learning and improvement endemic throughout your organization?

902. Are all employees including salespersons made aware that they must report all complaints received from any source for inclusion in the complaint handling system?

903. Health and safety arrangements; stress management workshops. How does your organization know that it provides a safe and healthy environment?

904. Quality is about improvement and accountability. The immediate questions that arise out of that statement are: (i) improvement on what, and (ii) accountable to whom?

905. Are adequate and conveniently located toilet facilities available for use by the employees?

906. What does an analysis of your organizations staff profile suggest in terms of its planning, and how is this being addressed?

907. Are the intentions consistent with external obligations (such as applicable laws)?

908. Are training programs documented?

909. Is your organizational structure established and each positions responsibility defined?

910. How does your organization know that its staffing profile is optimally aligned with the capability requirements implicit (or explicit) in its Strategic Plan?

911. How does your organization know that its staff are presenting original work, and properly acknowledging the work of others?

912. Can your organization demonstrate exactly how and why results were achieved?

913. How does your organization know that its system

for examining work done is appropriately effective and constructive?

914. How does your organization ensure that equipment is appropriately maintained and producing valid results?

3.6 Team Directory: Business Cost Optimization

915. How do unidentified risks impact the outcome of the Business Cost Optimization project?

916. Where will the product be used and/or delivered or built when appropriate?

917. Who should receive information (all stakeholders)?

918. Have you decided when to celebrate the Business Cost Optimization projects completion date?

919. Process decisions: do job conditions warrant additional actions to collect job information and document on-site activity?

920. Decisions: is the most suitable form of contract being used?

921. Why is the work necessary?

922. How will the team handle changes?

923. When will you produce deliverables?

924. Process decisions: are all start-up, turn over and close out requirements of the contract satisfied?

925. Process decisions: how well was task order work performed?

926. Timing: when do the effects of communication take place?

927. Who will write the meeting minutes and distribute?

928. Do purchase specifications and configurations match requirements?

929. How will you accomplish and manage the objectives?

930. Who will be the stakeholders on your next Business Cost Optimization project?

931. Who are the Team Members?

932. Who will talk to the customer?

933. Is construction on schedule?

934. When does information need to be distributed?

3.7 Team Operating Agreement: Business Cost Optimization

935. Communication protocols: how will the team communicate?

936. Do you upload presentation materials in advance and test the technology?

937. Do you vary your voice pace, tone and pitch to engage participants and gain involvement?

938. To whom do you deliver your services?

939. Did you delegate tasks such as taking meeting minutes, presenting a topic and soliciting input?

940. Must your team members rely on the expertise of other members to complete tasks?

941. Are there more than two native languages represented by your team?

942. Is compensation based on team and individual performance?

943. Conflict resolution: how will disputes and other conflicts be mediated or resolved?

944. Reimbursements: how will the team members be reimbursed for expenses and time commitments?

945. What resources can be provided for the team

in terms of equipment, space, time for training, protected time and space for meetings, and travel allowances?

946. Do you ask participants to close laptops and place mobile devices on silent on the table while the meeting is in progress?

947. What are some potential sources of conflict among team members?

948. Do team members need to frequently communicate as a full group to make timely decisions?

949. The method to be used in the decision making process; Will it be consensus, majority rule, or the supervisor having the final say?

950. Do you listen for voice tone and word choice to understand the meaning behind words?

951. Are there more than two national cultures represented by your team?

952. Have you set the goals and objectives of the team?

953. How will you resolve conflict efficiently and respectfully?

3.8 Team Performance Assessment: Business Cost Optimization

954. To what degree do all members feel responsible for all agreed-upon measures?

955. To what degree does the teams work approach provide opportunity for members to engage in results-based evaluation?

956. How hard did you try to make a good selection?

957. What structural changes have you made or are you preparing to make?

958. To what degree can the team measure progress against specific goals?

959. To what degree are the teams goals and objectives clear, simple, and measurable?

960. To what degree do team members understand one anothers roles and skills?

961. To what degree will the approach capitalize on and enhance the skills of all team members in a manner that takes into consideration other demands on members of the team?

962. To what degree are staff involved as partners in the improvement process?

963. How do you encourage members to learn from

each other?

964. Individual task proficiency and team process behavior: what is important for team functioning?

965. How does Business Cost Optimization project termination impact Business Cost Optimization project team members?

966. To what degree can team members meet frequently enough to accomplish the teams ends?

967. What are teams?

968. To what degree do members understand and articulate the same purpose without relying on ambiguous abstractions?

969. Do you give group members authority to make at least some important decisions?

970. To what degree does the teams purpose contain themes that are particularly meaningful and memorable?

971. To what degree are the members clear on what they are individually responsible for and what they are jointly responsible for?

972. To what degree are sub-teams possible or necessary?

973. To what degree are the goals realistic?

3.9 Team Member Performance Assessment: Business Cost Optimization

974. What stakeholders must be involved in the development and oversight of the performance plan?

975. What resources do you need?

976. Verify business objectives. Are they appropriate, and well-articulated?

977. To what degree do team members articulate the teams work approach?

978. How is performance assessment used in making future award decisions including options and extend/compete decisions?

979. What types of learning are targeted (e.g., cognitive, affective, psychomotor, procedural)?

980. To what extent are systems and applications (e.g., game engine, mobile device platform) utilized?

981. How will they be formed?

982. In what areas would you like to concentrate your knowledge and resources?

983. How often are assessments to be conducted?

984. What steps have you taken to improve

performance?

985. Are any validation activities performed?

986. What evaluation results did you have?

987. What are the standards or expectations for success?

988. How is your organizations Strategic Management System tied to performance measurement?

989. What evaluation results do you have?

990. What are the staffs preferences for training on technology-based platforms?

991. How effective is training that is delivered through technology-based platforms?

3.10 Issue Log: Business Cost Optimization

992. Is the issue log kept in a safe place?

993. Which team member will work with each stakeholder?

994. Is there an important stakeholder who is actively opposed and will not receive messages?

995. Are there common objectives between the team and the stakeholder?

996. Are stakeholder roles recognized by your organization?

997. In your work, how much time is spent on stakeholder identification?

998. Are you constantly rushing from meeting to meeting?

999. What is a Stakeholder?

1000. Which stakeholders can influence others?

1001. In classifying stakeholders, which approach to do so are you using?

1002. Persistence; will users learn a work around or will they be bothered every time?

1003. Who is the issue assigned to?

1004. What steps can you take for positive relationships?

1005. What is the impact on the risks?

1006. Why multiple evaluators?

1007. What is the stakeholders level of authority?

4.0 Monitoring and Controlling Process Group: Business Cost Optimization

1008. Propriety: who needs to be involved in the evaluation to be ethical?

1009. Did it work?

1010. What are the goals of the program?

1011. Are the necessary foundations in place to ensure the sustainability of the results of the programme?

1012. Who are the Business Cost Optimization project stakeholders?

1013. What resources are necessary?

1014. How should needs be met?

1015. Do the products created live up to the necessary quality?

1016. User: who wants the information and what are they interested in?

1017. Is there sufficient funding available for this?

1018. If a risk event occurs, what will you do?

1019. What departments are involved in its daily

operation?

1020. How was the program set-up initiated?

1021. Specific - is the objective clear in terms of what, how, when, and where the situation will be changed?

1022. Just how important is your work to the overall success of the Business Cost Optimization project?

1023. What areas does the group agree are the biggest success on the Business Cost Optimization project?

1024. What are the deliverables?

1025. Is there sufficient time allotted between the general system design and the detailed system design phases?

1026. How many potential communications channels exist on the Business Cost Optimization project?

4.1 Project Performance Report: Business Cost Optimization

1027. To what degree are the tasks requirements reflected in the flow and storage of information?

1028. To what degree does the informal organization make use of individual resources and meet individual needs?

1029. To what degree is there centralized control of information sharing?

1030. To what degree will team members, individually and collectively, commit time to help themselves and others learn and develop skills?

1031. What is the degree to which rules govern information exchange between individuals within your organization?

1032. To what degree will new and supplemental skills be introduced as the need is recognized?

1033. Next Steps?

1034. To what degree does the teams approach to its work allow for modification and improvement over time?

1035. To what degree do the goals specify concrete team work products?

1036. What degree are the relative importance and priority of the goals clear to all team members?

1037. To what degree will each member have the opportunity to advance his or her professional skills in all three of the above categories while contributing to the accomplishment of the teams purpose and goals?

1038. To what degree is the information network consistent with the structure of the formal organization?

1039. To what degree does the funding match the requirement?

1040. What is in it for you?

1041. To what degree are the goals ambitious?

4.2 Variance Analysis: Business Cost Optimization

1042. What causes selling price variance?

1043. What is the budgeted cost for work scheduled?

1044. Does the scheduling system identify in a timely manner the status of work?

1045. Historical experience?

1046. How are material, labor, and overhead variances calculated and recorded?

1047. Is there a logical explanation for any variance?

1048. Are data elements reconcilable between internal summary reports and reports forwarded to the stakeholders?

1049. What can be the cause of an increase in costs?

1050. Other relevant issues of Variance Analysis -selling price or gross margin?

1051. Did your organization lose existing customers and/or gain new customers?

1052. Are there changes in the overhead pool and/or organization structures?

1053. Are the bases and rates for allocating costs from

each indirect pool consistently applied?

1054. Are management actions taken to reduce indirect costs when there are significant adverse variances?

1055. Do the rates and prices remain constant throughout the year?

1056. Are meaningful indicators identified for use in measuring the status of cost and schedule performance?

1057. What costs are avoidable if one or more customers are dropped?

1058. Did an existing competitor change strategy?

4.3 Earned Value Status: Business Cost Optimization

1059. Validation is a process of ensuring that the developed system will actually achieve the stakeholders desired outcomes; Are you building the right product? What do you validate?

1060. Where is evidence-based earned value in your organization reported?

1061. How much is it going to cost by the finish?

1062. Verification is a process of ensuring that the developed system satisfies the stakeholders agreements and specifications; Are you building the product right? What do you verify?

1063. How does this compare with other Business Cost Optimization projects?

1064. When is it going to finish?

1065. Where are your problem areas?

1066. Are you hitting your Business Cost Optimization projects targets?

1067. What is the unit of forecast value?

1068. Earned value can be used in almost any Business Cost Optimization project situation and in almost any Business Cost Optimization project environment. it may be used on large Business Cost Optimization projects, medium sized Business Cost Optimization projects, tiny Business Cost Optimization projects (in cut-down form), complex and simple Business Cost Optimization projects and in any market sector. some people, of course, know all about earned value, they have used it for years - but perhaps not as effectively as they could have?

1069. If earned value management (EVM) is so good in determining the true status of a Business Cost Optimization project and Business Cost Optimization project its completion, why is it that hardly any one uses it in information systems related Business Cost Optimization projects?

4.4 Risk Audit: Business Cost Optimization

1070. Is Business Cost Optimization project scope stable?

1071. Why do audits fail?

1072. Are risk assessments documented?

1073. Are procedures developed to respond to foreseeable emergencies and communicated to all involved?

1074. Does your organization have any policies or procedures to guide its decision-making (code of conduct for the board, conflict of interest policy, etc.)?

1075. Where will the next scandal or adverse media involving your organization come from?

1076. Do you have a realistic budget and do you present regular financial reports that identify how you are going against that budget?

1077. How effective are your risk controls?

1078. For paid staff, does your organization comply with the minimum conditions for employment and/or the applicable modern award?

1079. How do you prioritize risks?

1080. If applicable; are compilers and code generators available and suitable for the product to be built?

1081. Are regular safety inspections made of buildings, grounds and equipment?

1082. Are all participants informed of safety issues?

1083. Are your rules, by-laws and practices non-discriminatory?

1084. Is the technology to be built new to your organization?

1085. Do you have written and signed agreements/contracts in place for each paid staff member?

1086. Do you have a mechanism for managing change?

1087. What programmatic and Fiscal information is being collected and analyzed?

1088. How do you govern assets?

1089. For this risk .. what do you need to stop doing, start doing and keep doing?

4.5 Contractor Status Report: Business Cost Optimization

1090. What was the actual budget or estimated cost for your organizations services?

1091. What process manages the contracts?

1092. How does the proposed individual meet each requirement?

1093. What was the budget or estimated cost for your organizations services?

1094. Who can list a Business Cost Optimization project as organization experience, your organization or a previous employee of your organization?

1095. What was the overall budget or estimated cost?

1096. How long have you been using the services?

1097. What are the minimum and optimal bandwidth requirements for the proposed solution?

1098. How is risk transferred?

1099. What was the final actual cost?

1100. Are there contractual transfer concerns?

1101. Describe how often regular updates are made to the proposed solution. Are corresponding regular updates included in the standard maintenance plan?

1102. What is the average response time for answering a support call?

1103. If applicable; describe your standard schedule for new software version releases. Are new software version releases included in the standard maintenance plan?

4.6 Formal Acceptance: Business Cost Optimization

1104. Did the Business Cost Optimization project manager and team act in a professional and ethical manner?

1105. What features, practices, and processes proved to be strengths or weaknesses?

1106. Was the client satisfied with the Business Cost Optimization project results?

1107. Did the Business Cost Optimization project achieve its MOV?

1108. Do you perform formal acceptance or burn-in tests?

1109. Was the Business Cost Optimization project goal achieved?

1110. Have all comments been addressed?

1111. What was done right?

1112. General estimate of the costs and times to complete the Business Cost Optimization project?

1113. Who would use it?

1114. What is the Acceptance Management Process?

1115. Was the sponsor/customer satisfied?

1116. How does your team plan to obtain formal acceptance on your Business Cost Optimization project?

1117. Was business value realized?

1118. What are the requirements against which to test, Who will execute?

1119. Does it do what Business Cost Optimization project team said it would?

1120. Was the Business Cost Optimization project work done on time, within budget, and according to specification?

1121. What can you do better next time?

1122. Does it do what client said it would?

1123. Do you buy-in installation services?

5.0 Closing Process Group: Business Cost Optimization

1124. What was learned?

1125. Was the user/client satisfied with the end product?

1126. Were sponsors and decision makers available when needed outside regularly scheduled meetings?

1127. Did the Business Cost Optimization project team have the right skills?

1128. Are there funding or time constraints?

1129. Were the outcomes different from the already stated planned?

1130. Is there a clear cause and effect between the activity and the lesson learned?

1131. How well did the team follow the chosen processes?

1132. Based on your Business Cost Optimization project communication management plan, what worked well?

1133. Just how important is your work to the overall success of the Business Cost Optimization project?

1134. What went well?

1135. What is an Encumbrance?

1136. When will the Business Cost Optimization project be done?

1137. What is the Business Cost Optimization project name and date of completion?

1138. What level of risk does the proposed budget represent to the Business Cost Optimization project?

1139. What were the actual outcomes?

1140. What will you do to minimize the impact should a risk event occur?

1141. What areas does the group agree are the biggest success on the Business Cost Optimization project?

5.1 Procurement Audit: Business Cost Optimization

1142. Is there a system in place to handle partial delivery of orders, back orders, and partial payments?

1143. Are approval limits covered in written procedures?

1144. Does the procurement function/unit have the ability to negotiate with customers and suppliers?

1145. Were standards, certifications and evidence required admissible?

1146. Were any additional works or deliveries admissible without the need for a new procurement procedure?

1147. Were the performance conditions under the contract comprehensive and unambiguous?

1148. Are there procedures to ensure that changes to purchase orders will be updated on the computer files?

1149. Are there systems for recording and managing stocks (where part of contract)?

1150. Is there a formal program of inservice training for personnel in the business management function?

1151. Does the procurement function/unit have the

ability to apply electronic procurement?

1152. Did the chosen procedure ensure competition and transparency?

1153. If an electronic auction or a dynamic purchasing system was used, did the tender documents specify details on access to information, electronic equipment used and connection specifications?

1154. Is there a procedure on requesting bids?

1155. Are required quality and service standards set?

1156. Has your organization taken a well-grounded decision about the procurement procedure chosen and has it documented the process?

1157. Where your organization engaged an expert, was the contract awarded in compliance with procurement regulations?

1158. Are incentives to deliver on time and in quantity properly specified?

1159. Was the payment made to the supplier/contractor within the time frames indicated in the contracts?

1160. Did you consider and evaluate alternatives, like bundling needs with other departments or grouping supplies in separate lots with different characteristics?

1161. Did additional works amount to no more than 50% of the initial contract?

5.2 Contract Close-Out: Business Cost Optimization

1162. Change in circumstances?

1163. Have all contract records been included in the Business Cost Optimization project archives?

1164. Change in attitude or behavior?

1165. Was the contract type appropriate?

1166. Has each contract been audited to verify acceptance and delivery?

1167. Parties: who is involved?

1168. Was the contract complete without requiring numerous changes and revisions?

1169. Why Outsource?

1170. How is the contracting office notified of the automatic contract close-out?

1171. How does it work?

1172. Have all acceptance criteria been met prior to final payment to contractors?

1173. Have all contracts been completed?

1174. Change in knowledge?

1175. What is capture management?

1176. Was the contract sufficiently clear so as not to result in numerous disputes and misunderstandings?

1177. Are the signers the authorized officials?

1178. How/when used ?

1179. Have all contracts been closed?

1180. What happens to the recipient of services?

1181. Parties: Authorized?

5.3 Project or Phase Close-Out: Business Cost Optimization

1182. In preparing the Lessons Learned report, should it reflect a consensus viewpoint, or should the report reflect the different individual viewpoints?

1183. Is the lesson based on actual Business Cost Optimization project experience rather than on independent research?

1184. Planned remaining costs?

1185. How often did each stakeholder need an update?

1186. Does the lesson educate others to improve performance?

1187. What stakeholder group needs, expectations, and interests are being met by the Business Cost Optimization project?

1188. What hierarchical authority does the stakeholder have in your organization?

1189. What is a Risk Management Process?

1190. What information did each stakeholder need to contribute to the Business Cost Optimization projects success?

1191. Who are the Business Cost Optimization project

stakeholders and what are roles and involvement?

1192. Who is responsible for award close-out?

1193. Planned completion date?

1194. Who controlled the resources for the Business Cost Optimization project?

1195. Complete yes or no?

1196. When and how were information needs best met?

1197. Were cost budgets met?

1198. What process was planned for managing issues/ risks?

5.4 Lessons Learned: Business Cost Optimization

1199. Who needs to learn lessons?

1200. What is your working hypothesis, if you have one?

1201. Do you conduct the engineering tests?

1202. How well was Business Cost Optimization project status communicated throughout your involvement in the Business Cost Optimization project?

1203. How well were Business Cost Optimization project issues communicated throughout your involvement in the Business Cost Optimization project?

1204. How useful do individuals find communications?

1205. How well were your expectations met regarding the extent of your involvement in the Business Cost Optimization project (effort, time commitments, etc.)?

1206. Under what legal authority did your organization head and program manager direct your organization and Business Cost Optimization project?

1207. How well did the scope of the Business Cost Optimization project match what was defined in the

Business Cost Optimization project Proposal?

1208. What report generation capability is needed?

1209. How long did redeployment take?

1210. What regulatory constraints impact the case?

1211. How effectively and timely was your organizational change impact identified and planned for?

1212. What skills did you need that were missing on this Business Cost Optimization project?

1213. What is the impact of tax policy?

1214. How timely was the training you received in preparation for the use of the product/service?

1215. What is the skill mix defined for the staffing?

1216. What are the funding priorities for intelligence?

1217. Where could you improve?

Index

ability 35, 88, 199, 261-262
abroad   140
accept   145
acceptable   52, 82, 100
acceptance   6, 131, 147, 149, 183, 231, 257-258, 263
accepted   116, 156, 188
accepting   215
access 2, 10-11, 20, 63, 147, 156, 188, 194, 199, 262
accomplish   8, 91, 109, 125, 137, 146, 167, 236, 240
accordance   181
according   36-37, 155, 176, 183, 207, 258
account   12, 35, 59, 190, 207, 226
accounting   196
accounts   161
accuracy   58, 182
accurate   11, 120, 149, 204
achievable   110
achieve   8, 63, 82-83, 112, 195, 206, 213, 251, 257
achieved   21, 86, 91, 110, 199, 233, 257
achieving   206
acquire   225
acquired   167, 195
across 56, 144
action 49, 56, 98-99, 105, 206, 222
actionable   48, 113
actions 20, 57, 106, 130, 142, 235, 250
active 182, 190, 219
actively   243
activities   24-25, 27, 37, 81, 102, 106, 130, 135, 139, 145,
147, 163-167, 170-172, 174, 176, 178, 180, 184-185, 208, 242
activity 3-4, 36, 43, 141, 157, 163, 165-168, 170-171, 173, 176, 178,
180, 184, 235, 259
actual 36, 59, 160, 180, 196, 255, 260, 265
actually   42, 82, 101, 251
addition   9, 129
additional   34-35, 65, 67, 72-73, 186, 208, 235, 261-262
additions   99
address   25, 84, 136, 141, 191, 217
addressed   141, 173, 202, 233, 257
addressing   35, 122

adequate   39, 156-157, 201, 217-218, 233
adequately   34, 141, 160, 163
Adjust 99, 101
adjusted   230
admissible   261
advance   206, 237, 248
advantage   63, 131
advantages   139, 150
adverse   250, 253
Advisory   216
affect 63, 66, 71, 118, 129, 134, 141, 146, 151, 153, 188, 206,
223, 228-229
affected   160, 183, 202, 208, 212, 221, 227
affecting   14, 21, 66
affective   241
affordable   90
against37, 104, 106, 177, 239, 253, 258
agenda   141
agendas   124
agents 194
aggregate   56
agreed   183
agreement   6, 110, 148, 183, 237
agreements   72, 87, 251, 254
aiming 112
alerts   99
aligned   24, 233
Alignment   164
aligns   145
alleged   1
alliance   86
allocate   114, 184
allocated   50, 53, 117, 161
allocating   160, 249
allotted   246
allowable   55
allowances   238
allowed   111, 174, 216
allows 11, 171
almost 251
already   123, 193, 224, 259
Although   135
altogether   209

always 11
Amazon   12
ambiguous   240
ambitious   248
amended   160
amount   24, 219, 262
amplify64, 108
analysis   3, 6, 13, 66, 69, 73-74, 76, 79, 84, 93, 139, 156,
164, 174, 187-188, 196-197, 199, 208, 210, 212, 227, 233, 249
analyze   2, 62, 68, 72
analyzed   82, 99, 160, 213, 254
analyzes   143
annual 188
annually   161
another   12, 158
anothers   239
answer 13-14, 18, 30, 47, 62, 78, 95, 107, 154, 191, 227
answered   29, 45, 61, 77, 94, 106, 132
answering   13, 256
anybody   141
anyone   43, 113, 121
anything   165, 173, 188, 230
appear   1
applicable   14, 100, 147, 196, 231, 233, 253-254, 256
applied   168, 232, 250
appointed   35, 38
approach   88, 90, 119, 156, 182, 224, 239, 241, 243, 247
approaches   79, 84, 202
approval   33, 128, 261
approvals   164, 201
approved   38, 70, 151, 156, 188, 201, 221, 228
approving   151
architect   154
Architects   8
archives   263
around109, 126, 220, 243
arriving145
articulate   240-241
asking 1, 8, 189, 195
assess   23, 34, 92, 96, 112, 145, 171, 226
assessed   80, 206
assessing   85, 96
Assessment   5-6, 10-11, 23, 147, 204, 206, 208, 239, 241

assets 55, 254
assign 22
assigned   43, 153, 159-161, 168, 200, 232, 244
assigning   174
Assignment   4, 196
assist   10, 68, 87, 104, 186, 197, 222, 230
assistant   8
associated   134, 160, 217
assuming   208
Assumption   3, 156
assurance   24, 198, 200-201, 214, 231
assure 232
attainable   37
attempted   43
attempting   97
attend 28
attendance   35
attendant   87
attended   35
attending   205
attention   14, 111
attitude   263
attitudes   225
attributes   3, 107, 167, 226
auction   262
audience   190, 220-221
audited   182, 263
auditing   19, 99, 118, 156, 196, 232
audits 253
auspices   9
author 1
authority   75, 148, 240, 244, 265, 267
authorized   144, 160-161, 196, 264
automatic   263
available   20, 27, 34, 43, 55, 65, 67, 104, 107, 165, 167, 184,
197, 200, 205, 207-210, 212, 233, 245, 254, 259
Average   14, 29, 45, 61, 77, 94, 106, 132, 178, 231, 256
averse 209
avoidable   250
avoidance   204
avoiding   205
awarded   262
background   12

backup 153
backward 228
balance 198
balanced 83
bandwidth 255
barriers 110, 203
baseline 4, 115, 145, 188-189
baselined 214, 218
baselines 33
basics 119
become 108, 123, 125, 151, 231
becomes 231
before 11, 43, 106, 166, 178, 182, 188
beginning 2, 17, 29, 45, 61, 77, 94, 106, 132
behavior 240, 263
Behaviors 198, 230
behind 238
belief 13, 18, 30, 47, 62, 78, 95, 107, 122
believable 110
believe 122
beneficial 192
benefit 1, 21, 84, 102, 139, 197
benefits 25, 49, 51, 53, 65, 74, 107-108, 110, 117, 119, 122, 136, 171
better 8, 33, 48, 84, 178-179, 187, 193, 230, 258
between 75, 134, 140, 142, 151, 160-161, 177, 197, 203, 215, 226, 243, 246-247, 249, 259
biased 211
biggest 54, 91, 193, 246, 260
blinding 66
Blokdyk 9
bother 58
bothered 243
bottleneck 165
bought 12
bounce 64
boundaries 36
bounds 36
Breakdown 3-4, 86, 154, 158-159, 174
briefed 38
Briefly 176
brings 39
broken 63

budget 86, 98, 100, 107, 161, 166, 178, 183, 218, 223, 253, 255, 258, 260
budgeted 59, 160, 196, 249
budgeting 160
budgets 18, 107, 160-161, 266
building 20, 100, 136, 175, 251
buildings 254
bundling 262
burn-in 257
Business 1-8, 10-16, 19-45, 47-50, 52-139, 141-149, 151, 153-161, 163-190, 192-194, 196-198, 200-202, 204, 206-212, 214-216, 218-220, 222-226, 228-230, 232, 235-237, 239-241, 243, 245-247, 249, 251-253, 255, 257-261, 263, 265-268
busywork 142
button 12
buy-in 120, 258
buyout 143
by-laws 254
calculate 171, 193
calculated 249
called 222
cannot 172, 185
capability 23, 137, 188, 233, 268
capable 8, 33, 196
capacities 117
capacity 20, 23, 92, 137, 141
capital 127
capitalize 62, 239
capture 48, 97, 264
captured 60, 71, 86, 115, 182, 200, 204, 214, 219
career 151, 198
careers 115
carried 64, 212
categories 248
category 45
caused 1, 56
causes 48, 54, 56, 62, 68, 70, 106, 144, 176, 212, 249
causing 21
celebrate 87, 235
center 48
centrally 83
certain 202
chaired 9

challenge   8, 230
challenges   110, 135
champions   195
change   5, 18, 28, 40, 48, 51, 65, 73, 75, 80, 90-91, 97, 117,
138, 144-145, 148, 159, 172, 184, 189, 194, 200, 220-221, 226, 228-
229, 250, 254, 263, 268
changed   25, 40, 107, 181, 186, 232, 246
changes   19, 33, 37-38, 53, 70, 80, 87-88, 99, 106, 109, 113,
131, 144-145, 148, 153, 155-157, 160, 175-176, 183, 188-190, 198,
226-228, 235, 239, 249, 261, 263
changing   99, 109, 139
channel   134
channels   149, 246
chargeable   196
charged   50, 160
Charter   2, 30, 42, 83, 136-137, 141, 164
charting   164
charts 64, 180
cheaper   48
checked   100, 102, 150
checklist   9
checklists   10, 164
choice 45, 130, 238
choose   13, 87
chosen212, 218, 223, 259, 262
circumvent   27
claimed   1
clarify 130
clarity 154
classes 146
clearly 13, 18, 27, 30-32, 44, 47, 62, 74, 78, 91, 95, 107, 150, 198
client   9, 12, 50, 112, 144, 257-259
clients 19, 45, 210
closed 98, 161, 218, 228, 264
closely 12, 180
Close-Out   6-7, 263, 265-266
closest 114
Closing6, 65, 259
Coaches   31
cognitive   241
colleague   114
colleagues   111, 116, 178
collect 69, 98, 186, 194, 235

collected	33, 43, 64, 67, 70, 75, 82, 254
collection	76, 194
collective	232
combine	84
coming	74, 216
command	103
comments	257
commit	204, 247
commitment	115, 141, 195
committed	180, 182, 200
committee	146, 182, 190, 216, 219
common	217, 243
community	178, 186-187, 212
companies	1, 9, 103, 177, 230
company	8, 47, 63, 108, 111, 113-114, 120, 125
compare	69, 92, 180, 251
compared	108
comparing	79
comparison	13
compatible	228
compelling	31
compete	241
competing	60
competitor	250
compilers	254
complain	193
complaint	232
complaints	207, 232
complete	1, 10, 13, 27, 32, 40-41, 167, 169, 172, 179, 193, 204, 207, 210, 237, 257, 263, 266
completed	14, 30, 41, 44-45, 165, 204, 263
completely	121
completing	131, 158, 172
completion	32, 43, 146, 161, 171, 183, 196, 235, 252, 260, 266
complex	8, 120, 190, 252
complexity	19, 53, 69, 154, 163, 226
compliance	20, 49-50, 53, 74, 87, 157, 191, 232, 262
comply	253
component	192
components	177, 182
compute	14
computer	261
computing	121

concept	91, 169, 194
concepts	190
concern	54, 86
concerns	19, 23, 114, 202, 255
concise	148
concrete	83, 247
condition	98
conditions	100, 144, 216, 235, 253, 261
conduct	253, 267
conducted	146, 192, 215, 218, 226-227, 241
confidence	171, 193, 205
confident	208
confirm	14
conflict	237-238, 253
conflicts	237
connecting	130
connection	262
consensus	238, 265
consider	21, 25, 27, 137, 262
considered	26-27, 59, 230
considers	63, 191
consist	160
consistent	42, 49, 71, 104, 142-143, 157, 162, 196, 233, 248
constant	250
constantly	243
constrain	161
Constraint	3, 156, 218
consultant	8
consulted	113, 202
consulting	56
consumers	107
contact	8, 183
contacts	117, 220
contain	26, 72, 98, 240
contained	1, 161
contains	10
content	42, 157, 231
contents	1-2, 10
context	32, 39-40
continual	12, 98, 103
continuous	67
contract	6, 146, 161, 183, 196-197, 225, 235, 261-264
contractor	6, 161, 176, 196-197, 255, 262

contracts   33, 72, 139, 160, 169, 183, 214, 254-255, 262-264
contribute   149, 265
control 2, 44, 59, 70, 86, 95, 97, 101-105, 148, 160-161, 164, 177, 186, 223, 226, 231, 247
controlled   266
controls   26, 65, 74, 84-85, 90, 99, 101-104, 172, 207, 253
convention   118
convey   1
cooperate   186
Copyright   1
correct47, 95, 143, 177
corrective   57, 106
correlate   192
correspond   10, 12
costing53
counting   108, 160
counts 108
course 40, 48, 252
covered   261
covering   10, 100
coworker   112
crashing   171
craziest   117
create 12, 26, 73, 108, 120, 154
created   64, 76, 138, 141, 143, 164, 182, 212, 219, 245
creating   8, 54
creative   20
creativity   92
credible   186
crisis   20
criteria 2, 5, 10, 12, 37, 43, 45, 66, 87, 92, 96, 119, 129, 133, 147, 149, 152, 180, 187, 214, 216, 263
CRITERION   2, 18, 30, 47, 62, 78, 95, 107
critical 33, 42, 45, 64, 99, 104, 134, 163, 165, 222-223, 231
criticism   76
cross-sell   120
crucial 65
crystal 14
culture 33, 66, 141, 199, 220
cultures   238
current37, 47, 59, 64, 69-70, 75, 93, 98, 109, 115-117, 122, 157, 160-161, 183, 198, 206-207, 209, 223, 226
currently   36, 127

custom28
customer   12, 24, 33, 35, 37-38, 43-44, 82, 98, 100, 112, 114, 123, 126, 136, 149, 154, 192, 204, 209-210, 236, 258
customers   1, 27, 42, 45, 48-49, 51, 53-54, 69-70, 105, 108, 110-111, 113-117, 124-125, 129-130, 169, 183, 191, 224, 249-250, 261
customize   220
cut-down   252
damage   1
Dashboard   10
dashboards   99
databases   194
day-to-day   103, 131, 169
deadlines   27, 125
deceitful   112
decide91, 190, 199
decided   87, 235
deciding   109
decision   6, 52, 74, 79, 81, 90-91, 196, 230-231, 238, 259, 262
decisions   80-81, 84, 89, 92-93, 96-97, 105, 134, 214, 219, 230, 235, 238, 240-241
decomposed 177
dedicate   197
dedicated   8
deeper   14
defect 146
defects   193
define 2, 30-31, 33, 71-72, 82, 147, 158, 193, 230
defined   13-14, 18, 21, 26, 30-36, 39-40, 43-45, 47, 62, 74, 78, 95, 107, 153-154, 156, 159-160, 163, 168, 176, 181, 198, 200, 233, 267-268
defines 25, 35-36, 175, 185
defining   8, 109, 154, 156
definite   98, 168
definition   22, 27, 31, 35, 38, 40, 156, 182, 214
degree   180, 205, 239-241, 247-248
delaying   49
delays 52
delegate   237
delegated   33
deletions   99
deliver 27, 45, 82, 110, 113, 179, 187, 237, 262

delivered   60, 119, 174, 188, 235, 242
deliveries   261
delivering   145, 206
delivers   175
delivery   59, 109, 142, 170, 261, 263
Delphi 177
demand   131
demands   239
department   8, 108, 145, 160, 197, 225
depend   225
dependent   109
depends   111
depict 171
deploy 105, 116
deployed   106
deploying   56
deployment   58
derive 96
Describe   151, 169, 255-256
described   1, 153, 160, 228
describing   45
deserving   225
design 1, 9, 12, 66-67, 86-87, 103, 119, 141, 156-157, 196-197, 210, 246
designated   216
designed   8, 12, 73, 81-82, 232
designing   8
desired34, 64, 82, 174, 189, 251
detail   82, 158
detailed   64-65, 160-161, 163, 165, 181-182, 201, 246
details 262
detect 100
determine   12-13, 125, 129, 164-166, 186, 200
determined   72, 129, 194-195, 214
detracting   119
develop   55, 78, 81-82, 86, 92, 143-144, 147, 158, 206, 247
developed   9, 12, 39, 41-42, 84, 87, 156-157, 161, 169, 177, 194, 200, 214, 228, 251, 253
developing   71, 93, 180
device 241
devices   232, 238
diagnose   211
diagram   4, 52, 68, 171-172

diagrams   58, 164, 190
Dictionary   3, 160
differ   180
difference   142, 177, 231
different   8, 26, 35, 37, 42, 68, 118, 129, 199, 220, 230, 259,
262, 265
difficult 76, 166-167, 170, 174
dilemma   128
direct   160, 196, 267
direction   40, 47, 144
directions   212
directly 1, 69-70, 135
Directory   6, 235
Disagree   13, 18, 30, 47, 62, 78, 95, 107
disaster   58
disclosure   103
discrete   160
discussion   128
display 169
displayed   33, 74, 178
disputes   237, 264
disruptive   73
distressed   232
distribute   236
divergent   142
Divided   29, 33, 45, 61, 77, 94, 106, 132
division 144
document   12, 41, 145, 148-149, 154, 157, 230, 235
documented 34, 82, 91, 96, 99, 102, 105, 135, 150, 156, 182,
188, 198, 200-201, 220, 233, 253, 262
documents   8, 157, 160, 192, 262
domains   79
dormant   117
Driver   73
drivers 50
drives   57
driving 114, 126
dropped   163, 250
Duration   4, 141, 155, 158, 176, 178
durations   36, 223
during 40, 89, 135, 144, 173, 210, 216, 220
dynamic   262
dynamics   34

earlier 111
earned   6, 176, 251-252
economic   211-212
economical   130
economy   88, 140, 223
edition 10
editorial   1
educate   265
education   25, 105
effect 209, 214, 259
effective   19, 112, 120, 126, 157, 179, 216, 231-232, 234, 242, 253
effects 59, 139, 160, 236
efficiency   76, 105
efficient   59, 79, 225
effort   41, 47, 52, 55, 120, 144, 161, 182, 197, 219, 267
efforts 43, 85
Electrical   157
electronic   1, 262
elements   12-13, 39, 71, 103, 129, 161, 197, 249
Elevator   150
elicit   195
eliminated   197
e-mail 149
embarking   31
embrace   220
emerging   68, 100
emphasis   230
employee   91, 118, 255
employees   26-27, 63, 116, 124, 127, 232-233
employers   138
employment   253
empower   8
empowered   193
enable 73
enablers   121
encourage   92, 105, 239
endemic   232
engage   129, 237, 239
engaged   262
engagement   49, 138
engine 241
Engineers   157

enhance   100, 239
enhanced   115
enhancing   106
enough   8, 70, 111, 126, 129, 149, 151, 240
ensure 36-37, 66, 87, 124, 126-128, 131, 142, 147, 157, 177, 191-192, 195, 198, 200, 227, 234, 245, 261-262
ensures   127
ensuring   11, 117, 251
entail   53
Enterprise   224
entire   180, 192
entities 51, 144
entity   1, 150
envisaged   142
equipment   26, 234, 238, 254, 262
equipped   43
equitably   33
equivalent   163
errors   127
escalated   184
especially   177
essential   88, 185
essentials   125
establish   78, 105, 186
estimate   52-53, 59, 176, 178, 205, 257
estimated   32, 43, 53, 59, 130, 186-187, 205, 255
estimates   4, 39, 52, 69, 176, 184, 196, 214, 218
estimating   4, 163, 178, 182, 186, 201
estimation   82, 141
etcetera   53
ethical 120, 191, 245, 257
ethics   210
ethnic 108
evaluate   87-88, 90, 163, 262
evaluating   87
evaluation   66, 85, 91, 103, 214, 217, 239, 242, 245
evaluators   217, 244
events 28, 81, 89, 136
everyday   63
everyone   32-33
everything   50, 230
evidence   14, 55, 206-207, 224, 261
evolution   47

evolve 96
exactly 233
examined 33
examining 234
Example 2, 10, 15, 70, 157
examples 8, 10, 12, 136
exceed 158
exceeding 48
excellence 8, 40
excellent 54
excess 161
exchange 247
exclude 80
execute 258
executed 229
Executing 5, 222
execution 105, 135
executive 8, 123, 219
exercise 23
existence 209
existing 12-13, 111, 136, 144, 153, 177, 249-250
expect 109, 144, 179, 183
expected 25, 36, 81, 122, 128, 144-145, 176-177, 223, 230
expend 55
expenses 237
experience 114, 119, 178, 208, 232, 249, 255, 265
experiment 114
expert 176, 262
expertise 84, 144, 197, 237
experts 33
explained 12
explicit 233
explore 68
explored 191
exposure 207
exposures 86
extend 241
extent 13, 19, 21, 42, 81, 142, 241, 267
external 43, 192, 200, 208, 233
facilitate 13, 68, 99
facilities 217, 233
facing 27, 128
factored 139

factors 52, 80, 119, 134, 137, 186, 222
failed   53
failing   206
failure   121, 131, 213
fairly   33
falling   163
familiar 10
fashion 1, 43, 204
feasible   52, 63, 123, 163, 186, 226
feature 11
features   257
feedback   2, 12, 43-44, 53
finalized   15
financial   56, 69, 74, 113, 126, 253
fingertips   11
finish   137, 165-166, 168, 172, 251
Fiscal   254
focused   200
focuses   134
follow   12, 102, 119, 122, 171, 259
followed   37, 164, 214
following   10, 13, 154
follow-up   141-142
for--and   104
forecast   251
forefront   124
forever 107
forget   11
formal 6, 120, 148, 161, 164, 183, 226, 248, 257-258, 261
formally   35, 207, 218
format 12
formed241
forming   219
formula   14, 109
Formulate   30
forward   123, 126
forwarded   197, 249
foster   107, 124, 206
frames 262
framework   103, 124, 194
freaky   129
frequency   43, 99, 118, 192, 194, 213
frequently   56, 145, 238, 240

friend   114, 128
frontiers   90
fulfill   117
full-blown   55
full-scale   86
fulltime 182, 200
function   201, 261
functional   161, 197
functions   69, 112, 129, 149, 153, 174, 198, 200, 208
funded188
funding   126, 128, 146, 245, 248, 259, 268
further 207
future   8, 51, 98, 100, 128, 144, 161, 206, 241
gained72, 103
gather 13, 32, 35-36, 40, 42-44, 47, 64, 72
gathered   41, 62-63, 68, 73-75
gathering   32, 39, 204
general   93, 177, 183, 246, 257
generally   225
generate   70, 73
generated   65, 196
generation   10, 268
generators   254
Gerardus   9
getting54, 145, 202, 230
global 88, 121
govern117, 247, 254
governance   25, 111, 198
government   177
graded   207
granted   188
graphical   180
graphics   26
graphs 10
greatest   84
ground74
grounds   254
grouping   262
groups 129, 140, 174, 183, 220, 224
growing   177
growth 66, 119, 170
guaranteed   36
guidance   1

guidelines   230
handle 173, 208, 212, 235, 261
handling   232
happen   24, 122, 170, 207, 212, 227
happened   144, 227
happening   121
happens   8, 12, 37, 57, 118, 125-126, 185, 187, 213, 264
hardest   59
hardly 252
hardware   147, 177
havent 108
having 238
hazards   212
Health 233
healthy   233
hearing   108
helping   8
Herzberg   176
hidden 58
higher 161
highest 26
high-level   30, 44, 136
highlight   198, 206
Highly 63
high-tech   123
hijacking   110
hiring   99
historical   176, 187, 249
history 167, 188
hitters 64
hitting 251
honest 120
hoping 137
horizon 116
humans   8
hypotheses   62
hypothesis   267
identified   1, 22, 24, 26, 35, 37, 65, 74-75, 83, 135, 146, 160-161, 163, 168, 176, 188, 193, 196-197, 201, 207, 215, 221, 230, 250, 268
identify 13, 27, 66, 68, 70, 86, 154, 186, 202, 211, 249, 253
ignore 19
imbedded   103

immediate   233
impact 5, 41, 51-54, 92, 120, 155, 188-189, 204, 206, 208, 210, 227-228, 235, 240, 244, 260, 268
impacted   57, 134, 153, 157, 220
impacts   51, 178, 205
implement   20, 55, 66, 95
implicit 127, 233
importance   248
important   19, 24, 42, 62, 69-70, 111, 118, 128-130, 155, 192, 220-221, 240, 243, 246, 259
improve   2, 12-13, 71, 78-79, 81-83, 85-86, 88-92, 135, 174, 241, 265, 268
improved   78, 91, 93, 102, 216, 232
improving   225
incentives   99, 262
incident   207
include   28, 80, 84, 145, 153, 165, 176
included   2, 10, 20, 50, 141, 149, 153, 179, 186, 222, 226, 256, 263
INCLUDES   11
including   23, 30-32, 56, 76, 86, 98-99, 103, 156, 208, 232, 241
inclusion   232
increase   81, 120, 190, 249
increased   110, 199
increasing   118, 230
incredible   210
incurred   49
incurring   160
in-depth   10, 13
indicate   98, 119
indicated   106, 262
indicators   22, 55, 57, 69-70, 73, 93, 99, 141, 190, 250
indirect   50, 160, 184, 250
indirectly   1
individual   1, 54, 135, 165, 198, 237, 240, 247, 255, 265
industrial   209
industry   108, 123, 140, 169, 200
infinite 121
influence   90, 121, 138, 203, 230-231, 243
informal   247
informed   115, 197, 254
ingrained   104

inherent   112
in-house   136
initial   44, 109, 180, 191, 262
initially 42, 147, 161
initiated   140, 186, 228, 246
Initiating   2, 131, 134
initiative   13, 194-195, 202
Innovate   78
innovation   54, 74, 76, 88, 103, 119, 124
innovative   179, 187, 222
in-process   70
inputs   35, 45, 53, 65, 105
inservice   261
inside   20
insight 67, 73
insights 10
inspection   207
inspired   129
instead 117, 196
Institute   157
instructed   148
insure   123
integral   192
integrate   98, 121, 144
integrated   135
integrity   26, 113, 228
intended   1, 83
INTENT 18, 30, 47, 62, 78, 95, 107
intention   1
intentions   233
interact   112
interest 118, 140, 213, 224, 253
interested   140, 245
interests   24, 265
interfaces   196
interim 125, 160
internal   1, 43, 66, 125, 134, 160-161, 192, 197, 207, 215,
218, 249
interpret   13-14
intervals   215, 218-219
interview   125
introduce   204
introduced   153, 247

invaluable   2, 12
invest   77
investment   49, 68
investor   56
invoices   182
involve 131
involved   20, 27, 45, 50, 66, 68-69, 93, 117, 150, 163, 182,
198, 201-202, 225, 239, 241, 245, 253, 263
involves   96, 148
involving   253
issues   19-20, 23, 29, 135, 137, 153, 157, 173, 184, 200, 206, 249,
254, 266-267
istoppers   206
iteration   200
itself   1, 23
jointly   240
judgment   1, 176
justified102, 219
justify   207
knowledge   12, 41, 43, 72, 84, 93, 97, 99-100, 102-103, 107,
110, 122, 220, 241, 263
languages   237
laptops   238
largely 64
largest 177
latest   10
leader 19, 66, 93, 209
leaders32, 64, 115-116
leadership   23, 31, 34, 88, 116, 141
learned   7, 97, 115, 195, 259, 265, 267
learning   100, 102-103, 231-232, 241
ledger 177
lesson   259, 265
lessons 7, 86, 97, 115, 195, 265, 267
letter   149
Leveling   168
levels   23, 26, 33, 69-70, 93, 100, 158, 161, 164, 195
leverage   37, 88, 97, 114, 178, 187
leveraged   43
liability 1, 204
licensed   1
lifecycle   50, 76, 192
lifecycles   84

lifestyle 140
Lifetime   11
likelihood   83, 86, 206-207
likely   80, 98, 114, 145, 210, 216, 230
limitation   54
limited 12
limits   261
Linked 35, 230
listed   1
listen   113, 124, 238
locally 83, 164, 214
located   164, 214, 233
logged 226
logical 172-173, 249
longer 103, 208
long-term   102, 123, 129
Looking   24
losing 53
losses 22, 35
lowest 172
magnitude   83
maintain   95, 113, 119, 135, 145, 188
maintained   234
majority   238
makers 91, 101, 259
making   19, 74, 79-80, 90, 115, 194-195, 238, 241
manage   31-32, 38, 58, 60, 66, 71, 81, 84, 89, 122, 127, 135,
137, 145, 151, 163, 169, 173, 180, 190, 202, 206, 216, 236
manageable 33, 89, 177, 182
managed   8, 64-65, 72, 83-84, 97, 104, 147, 155, 176, 209,
214
management 1, 3-5, 10, 12-13, 21, 24, 30-31, 50, 65, 68, 70-71,
75, 79-81, 83, 86, 89, 93, 111, 114, 122, 126, 141, 143-145, 147,
153-157, 161, 163-164, 168, 174, 176-177, 180, 182-185, 188-190,
194-195, 200, 202, 204, 207, 211, 214, 218, 220, 222-224, 233, 242,
250, 252, 257, 259, 261, 264-265
manager   8, 13, 20, 37, 43, 110, 135, 143, 225, 257, 267
managers   2, 133, 143, 182, 208
manages   85, 89, 255
managing   2, 82, 133-134, 138, 148, 218, 232, 254, 261, 266
mandatory   228
manner   22, 89, 134, 157, 162, 196, 214, 226, 239, 249, 257
mantle 113

Manual   232
Mapping   64, 66, 71
margin 249
market 20, 169-170, 223, 252
marketer   8
marketing   107, 149, 191
markets   26, 140
Maslow   176
Master 181
material   136, 161, 170, 193, 217, 249
materials   1, 237
matrices   151
Matrix 3-5, 139, 151, 196-197, 210
matter 33, 55, 57
matters   231
maximizing   114
McClellan   176
McGregor   176
meaning   238
meaningful   49, 130, 240, 250
measurable   37-38, 239
measure   2, 13, 19, 23, 37, 41, 47-52, 54, 56-57, 59-60, 74, 76, 78, 84, 87, 94-95, 97, 105, 136, 141-142, 186-187, 189-190, 192, 239
measured   23, 48, 51, 53, 55, 59-60, 82, 105-106
measures   52, 54-56, 58, 69-70, 75-76, 93, 98-99, 190, 212, 222, 239
measuring   106, 250
mechanical   1
mechanism   254
mechanisms   142, 194
mediated   237
medium   252
meeting   37, 100, 182, 198, 214, 224, 236-238, 243
meetings   35-36, 38, 41, 205, 214-215, 218, 230, 238, 259
megatrends   123
member   5-6, 34, 125, 224, 241, 243, 248, 254
members   31, 33, 36, 41, 43, 65, 104, 142, 145, 153-154, 163-164, 182, 198, 200-202, 214, 218, 227, 236-241, 247-248
memorable   240
mentors   209
message   99
messages   243

method   52, 191, 238
methods   43-44, 52, 154, 156, 187
metrics 4, 36, 67, 99, 136, 163, 188, 192-193
milestone   3, 136, 169, 215, 218
milestones   30, 138, 168, 196
minimize   260
minimizing   76, 114
minimum   253, 255
minority   24
minutes   37, 182, 214, 236-237
missed 53, 108
missing 67, 115, 167-168, 268
mission 63, 118
mitigate   87, 206
mitigating   215
mitigation   139, 146, 204-205
mix-ups   232
mobile 238, 241
modeling   64
models 20, 50, 67, 114
modern   253
modified   105
moment   118
moments   65
momentum   108, 122
monetary   21
monitor   95-98, 102, 186, 201
monitored   99, 104-105, 166, 176, 178, 183
monitoring   6, 97, 99, 102-103, 105-106, 148, 164, 173, 180,
245
months 91
motivate   118
motivated   200
motivation   27, 101
motive 195
moving   123
multiple   214, 244
narrative   191
narrow 68
national   142, 212, 222, 238
native 237
nearest   14

necessary   63, 67-68, 73, 80, 113-114, 141-142, 186, 189-190, 201, 204, 235, 240, 245
needed   19-21, 24, 27-28, 35, 65, 69, 77, 96-97, 99, 105, 141, 156, 179, 184, 200, 203, 214, 259, 268
negative   115, 180
negatively   206
negotiate   112, 261
negotiated   110
neither 1
network   4, 171-172, 248
networks   177
Neutral 13, 18, 30, 47, 62, 78, 95, 107
nominated   221
Non-valid   210
normal 104
notice 1, 141
noticing   231
notified   220, 263
number   29, 45, 52, 61, 77, 94, 106, 132, 174, 193, 269
numbers   118
numerous   263-264
objection   26
objective   8, 196-197, 230, 246
objectives   21, 24, 30, 35, 39, 63, 96, 98, 112-113, 119, 130, 145, 149, 164, 176-177, 200, 206, 213, 215, 224, 236, 238-239, 241, 243
observe   198
observed   84
obsolete   123
obstacles   27, 179, 187
obtain 113, 258
obtained   43, 201
obtaining   53
obviously   14
occurred   191
occurring   88
occurs 20, 58, 106, 134, 142, 245
offerings   69, 92
office   154, 216, 224, 263
officers 217
officials 264
onboarding   163
one-time   8

ongoing   80, 105, 166, 178
on-going   146, 201
online 12
on-site 235
opened   161
operate   188, 212
operates   123
operating   6, 48, 60, 104, 227, 237
operation   101, 179, 188, 246
operations   13, 98-99, 104, 106, 188, 232
operators   102
opponent   230
opposed   243
opposite   122-123
opposition   118
optimal   79, 84, 93, 255
optimally   233
optimize   90, 106
optimized   108
option 130
options 20, 207, 241
orderly 232
orders 261
orient 100
origin 150
original 160, 163, 181, 204, 230, 233
originate   101, 202
others 186, 191, 197, 202-203, 207, 210, 214, 230, 233, 243, 247, 265
otherwise   1
outcome   14, 135, 137, 147, 174, 235
outcomes   85, 90, 106, 131, 141, 179, 187, 251, 259-260
outlined   96
output 37, 64, 66, 69, 71-76, 98, 100
outputs   45, 65-67, 71, 105, 141, 173
outside 92, 259
outsource   72, 177, 263
outweigh   53
overall 13-14, 24, 59, 98, 116, 149, 156, 171, 190, 193, 231, 246, 255, 259
overcome   179, 187
overhead   160-161, 249
overlooked   185, 222

oversight 75, 182, 190, 219, 241
overtime 167
owners 159
ownership 31, 97
package 161
packages 160
paradigms 116
paragraph 116
parallel 171
parameters 104
Pareto 64, 164
partial 261
particular 70
Parties 86, 263-264
partners 27, 45, 86, 111, 116, 124, 142, 169, 239
patterns 92
paycheck 113
paying 111
payment 164, 182, 214, 262-263
payments 183, 261
pending 228
people 8, 22, 54-55, 68, 76, 84, 93, 97, 105, 112, 114-117, 124-125, 127, 193, 205, 207, 210, 212, 220, 225, 252
perceive 127
percent 111
percentage 151
perception 78-79, 120
perform 22, 33, 35, 43, 147, 157, 174, 213, 257
performed 80, 151, 166, 177, 184, 196, 235, 242
performing 135
perhaps 25, 252
period 82
periodic 146
permission 1
person 1, 24, 140, 145, 169, 196
personal 121
personally 151
personnel 21, 75, 99, 163, 172, 194-195, 208, 211, 261
pertaining 135
pertinent 99
phases 50, 134, 168, 246
pitfalls 112
placed 217

planet 97
planned   96, 102, 104, 165, 183, 218, 259, 265-266, 268
planners   101
planning   3, 10, 104-105, 137, 141-145, 161, 172-174, 208, 211, 224, 233
platform   241
platforms   242
players 78
pocket 179
pockets   179
points   29, 45, 61, 73, 77, 94, 106, 131, 194, 196
policies   144, 199, 221, 232, 253
policy 39, 81, 101, 173, 253, 268
political   40, 121, 203, 210
portfolio   129
portfolios   202
portray 64
position   198
positioned   186
positions   233
positive   91, 108, 115, 144, 220, 244
positively   206
possible   49, 53, 68, 70, 89, 95, 121, 130, 146, 155, 197, 240
potential   26, 52, 83, 87-88, 90, 116, 119, 123, 150, 203, 213, 238, 246
practical   63, 78, 95, 224-225
practice   211
practiced   135
practices   1, 12, 76, 92, 97, 99, 143, 254, 257
precaution 1
precede   171
predicting   106
prediction   167
predictive   174
predictor   174
predictors   226
pre-filled   10
prepare   198-199, 214
prepared   217
preparing   239, 265
presence   139
present   100, 119, 128, 253
presented   27

presenting   233, 237
preserve   35
preserved   71
prevailing   209
prevent   50, 145, 206, 232
preventive   212
prevents   19
previous   43, 135, 193, 255
previously   140, 144, 207, 228
prices 250
primarily   200
primary   55, 147, 163
printing   9
priorities   50, 56, 60, 188, 268
prioritize   191, 253
priority 54, 58, 168, 248
privacy   34, 143, 192
probably   174
problem   18-22, 25, 27-28, 30, 37, 42-43, 55, 63, 72, 145,
148, 150, 225, 251
problems   20-21, 23-24, 26-27, 81-82, 88, 106, 119, 192, 217
procedural   241
procedure   227, 261-262
procedures   12, 82, 96, 102, 104-105, 156, 173, 176, 181, 183,
190-191, 194, 221, 231, 253, 261
proceed   196, 208
proceeding   178, 181
process   1-6, 8, 12, 30, 35, 37, 39, 42, 44-45, 59, 63-77, 84,
87, 95-98, 100-105, 134-135, 141-142, 144, 148, 151, 154-157, 163,
173, 176, 189, 191, 194-195, 201, 204, 211, 216, 219, 222, 230,
232, 235, 238-240, 245, 251, 255, 257, 259, 262, 265-266
processes   59, 62-63, 65-66, 68-73, 75-76, 99, 103, 135, 156-
157, 164, 200, 222-223, 226, 229, 232, 257, 259
procuring   222
produce   75, 173, 185, 223, 225, 235
produced   69, 91
producing   151, 234
product   1, 12, 59, 69-70, 122, 136, 146, 153-154, 156, 169-
170, 188-189, 192, 204, 212, 224-225, 235, 251, 254, 259, 268
production   38, 80, 110
productive   197
products   1, 25, 54, 111, 127, 136, 139, 141-142, 147, 151,
189, 193, 222, 224, 245, 247

profile 206, 233
program   20, 50, 100, 141-143, 206, 222, 245-246, 261, 267
programme   245
programs   144, 202, 225, 233
progress   38, 48, 87, 98, 115, 127, 136, 142, 145, 164, 183,
186, 194-195, 222-223, 238-239
project 2-4, 6-8, 10, 21-22, 28, 41, 55, 65, 69, 76, 79, 96, 104, 109-
111, 120-121, 128-131, 133-138, 141-149, 151, 153-159, 163-172,
174-190, 193, 197-198, 200-202, 204, 206-211, 214-215, 218-219,
222-225, 228-229, 235-236, 240, 245-247, 251-253, 255, 257-260,
263, 265-268
projected   160-161, 188
projects   2, 50, 111-112, 133, 142, 144, 151, 154-155, 158,
183, 188, 190, 202, 207, 209, 224, 235, 251-252, 265
promote   54, 76
promotion   199
promptly   184
proofing   84
proper 103, 164
properly   12, 32, 43, 160, 227, 232-233, 262
Proposal   216, 268
proposals   101
proposed   20, 53, 81, 85, 144, 147, 149, 255, 260
Propriety   245
protect   74, 116, 143
protected   71, 238
protection   114
protocols   192, 237
proved 257
provide   20, 67, 125-126, 128, 138, 148, 161, 177, 179, 185,
187, 192, 196, 239
provided   9, 14, 96, 157, 201, 216, 237
providers   86, 214
provides   169, 174, 233
providing   103, 138
provision   231
provokes   221
public 141
published   221
publisher   1
pulled 111
purchase   10, 12, 214, 216, 236, 261
purchased   12

purchasing 262
purpose 2, 12, 118, 136, 153, 174, 186, 189, 240, 248
purposes 137
pushing 129
qualified 33, 62-63, 65
qualifies 63, 72
qualify 51, 75-76
qualities 24
quality 1, 4, 6, 12, 24, 56, 58-59, 67-69, 101, 130, 134, 141-142, 155, 164, 183, 190-195, 198-201, 214, 222, 231-233, 245, 262
quantified 102
quantify 51
quantities 217
quantity 262
question 13-14, 18, 30, 47, 62, 78, 95, 107, 127, 195
questions 8, 10, 13, 63, 154, 202, 217, 233
quickly 13, 64, 70, 184, 204
radically 73
ranking 211
rather 114, 265
rational 196
reached 25
reaching 112
reactivate 117
readiness 38
readings 102
realistic 25, 131, 240, 253
realize 60
realized 122, 258
really 8, 19, 39, 148
reason 114, 122, 207, 220
reasonable 89, 131, 144, 215, 218
reasons 31, 177, 192
recasts 184
receive 10-11, 43, 51, 216, 220, 235, 243
received 38, 117, 163, 232, 268
recently 12, 123
recipient 21, 264
recognised 80
recognize 2, 18, 20-22, 26, 81, 87, 92
recognized 20-22, 24, 26, 28, 70, 243, 247
recognizes 20
recommend 114, 128, 153, 202

recorded 249
recording 1, 190, 261
records 65, 125, 190, 196, 263
recovery 156, 180
recurrence 213
redefine 25, 45
re-design 63
reduce 48, 53, 156, 250
reduced 212
reducing 100, 118
references 269
reflect 72, 95, 100, 157, 160, 265
reflected 247
reform 58, 101, 123, 128
reforms 20, 52-53
regard 142
regarding 113, 121, 191, 225, 267
Register 2, 5, 138, 206-207
regret 79
regular 38, 70, 253-255
regularly 35-36, 41, 259
regulatory 20, 191, 268
reimbursed 237
reject 220
relate 62, 176, 223, 228
related 20, 56, 72, 96, 147, 198, 202, 252
relating 188
relation 25, 89, 118
relations 206, 209
relative 98, 248
relatively 120
release 200
releases 256
relevant 12, 37, 51, 67, 103, 120, 141, 188, 208, 249
reliable 43, 213
relocation 143
relying 240
remain 40, 250
remaining 187, 265
remunerate 91
repair 146
repeat 135, 141
rephrased 12

replace 136
replaced 142
replanning 160
report 5-6, 88, 102, 145, 164, 169, 207, 224, 232, 247, 255, 265, 268
reported 251
reporting 75, 96, 148, 160, 192
reports 51, 95, 138, 143, 146, 163, 184, 196-197, 205, 249, 253
represent 82, 189, 260
reproduced 1
Reputation 113, 139
request 5, 63, 148, 188-189, 226, 228-229
requested 1, 80, 189, 216, 228
requesting 262
requests 216, 226
require 55, 73, 105, 136, 161, 173, 208
required 23, 36, 38, 41, 75, 79-80, 85, 139, 149, 157, 167, 194, 209, 220, 261-262
requiring 138, 263
research 20, 127, 170, 265
resemble 217
reserved 1
reside 81, 216
resolution 67, 237
resolve 22-23, 238
resolved 184, 204, 237
resource 4-5, 112, 134, 141, 168, 173-174, 182, 200, 205, 223-224
resources 2, 10, 19, 25-27, 34, 39, 43, 58, 64, 85-86, 99, 104, 112, 114, 117, 121, 135, 150, 157, 167, 172, 178, 187, 189, 201, 218, 237, 241, 245, 247, 266
respect 1
respond 253
responded 14
responding 207
response 20, 98, 103, 106, 256
responses 115, 217
responsive 178, 186
result 65, 82, 91, 153, 186, 189-190, 202, 228, 232, 264
resultant 216
resulted 105
resulting 74, 160

results   10, 36, 45, 69, 78, 81, 83, 87-88, 90, 92, 96, 99, 142-143, 186, 190, 194, 196-197, 222-223, 233-234, 242, 245, 257
Retain 107
retained   75
retrospect   111
return 91, 126, 171
revenue   23, 48
revenues   55
review 12-13, 38, 68, 147, 172, 192, 207, 226, 232
reviewed   39, 177, 207, 219
reviews 12, 146, 164, 196-197, 204, 215, 218
revised 69, 105
revisions   216, 263
revisit   231
reward 54, 71, 225
rewarded   26
rewards   99
rework 48, 57
rights   1
roadblocks   146
routine 101
rushing 243
safely   212
safety 127, 233, 254
sample 217
sampling   164
sanitized   156
satisfied   115, 148, 235, 257-259
satisfies 251
satisfying   129
savings 39, 57, 60, 69
scalable   84
scaled 163
scandal   253
scenario   35, 39
schedule   3-4, 36, 52, 86, 98, 124, 142, 146-147, 162-164, 176, 180-181, 188, 196-197, 200, 205, 214, 218, 228, 236, 250, 256
scheduled   146, 249, 259
Schedules   172, 216
scheduling   160, 163, 182, 201, 249
scheme 98
Scorecard   2, 14-16
scorecards   99

Scores 16
scoring 12
seamless   123
second   14
secondary   163
section 14, 29, 45, 61, 77, 94, 106, 131-132
sector 252
securing   48, 129
security   19, 72, 86, 96, 101, 138, 156, 228
segmented   37
segments   42, 129
select 67, 98
selected   93, 143, 186-187, 220
selecting   129
selection   5, 216-217, 239
sellers   1
selling   114, 230, 249
-selling 249
senior   111, 116
sensitive   34, 49
separate   262
sequence   165, 172
sequencing   123, 214
series   13
serious 204
seriously   139
service 1-2, 8-9, 12, 59, 78-79, 86, 153, 169-170, 188, 216, 224-225, 262, 268
services   1, 9, 54, 56, 59, 111, 124, 126, 139-140, 177, 185, 222, 237, 255, 258, 264
session 161
setbacks   64
setting 112, 131
set-up 246
several 9, 68
severance   232
severely   63
shared 103, 186
sharing 93, 100, 247
shifts   20

should 8, 23, 27-28, 41-42, 44, 51, 58-59, 67, 70, 72, 75, 77, 87, 91-92, 96, 105, 110, 112, 120, 124, 126, 137-138, 142, 153, 155, 165-167, 169, 174, 178, 181, 197-199, 207-208, 210, 212, 216-217, 222, 227, 235, 245, 260, 265   .
showing   141
sigmas 134
signature   124
signatures   173
signed 254
signers 264
silent   238
similar 41, 43, 64, 69, 92, 167, 188, 209
simple 120, 239, 252
simply 10, 12
single   116, 185
single-use   8
situation   23, 47, 141, 210, 246, 251
situations   99
skeptical   107
skills   23, 26, 74, 107, 110, 128, 184, 200, 207, 210, 223, 239, 247-248, 259, 268
slippage   209
smallest   18, 91
social   107, 212
societal   117
software   135, 147, 149, 156, 177, 217, 219, 222, 256
solicit 44
soliciting   237
solution   54, 63, 67, 78-82, 84-89, 92-93, 95, 154, 212, 255
solutions   55, 79, 82, 87, 90, 98, 144
solved 28, 145
Someone   8
something   156, 189
Sometimes   55
source 5, 128, 213, 216-217, 232
sources   44, 64, 68, 149, 211, 238
special 41, 96, 137
specific   10, 23, 37-39, 68, 122, 157, 166-167, 170, 173-174, 198, 200, 216, 220, 224, 229, 239, 246
specified   112, 160, 212, 262
specify 247, 262
Speech   150
spoken 123

sponsor   24, 258
sponsors   27, 194, 259
spread 99, 104
stability 145, 153   ·
stable   210, 253
staffed 34
staffing 23, 99, 144-145, 233, 268
staffs   242
stages 143
standard   8, 100, 135, 173, 192, 256
standards   1, 12-13, 98, 100, 102, 104, 156-157, 161, 190, 192-
193, 228, 242, 261-262
started 10
starting 13
start-up   235
stated 129, 150, 193, 259
statement   3, 13, 81-82, 153-154, 157, 188, 233
statements   14, 29-30, 37, 45, 61, 72, 77, 94, 106, 132, 148,
176, 195
status   5-6, 76, 145, 148, 163-164, 183, 206, 215, 218-219, 224,
226, 249-252, 255, 267
steady 59
steering   146, 182, 190, 219
stocks   261
storage   194, 232, 247
stored 147
stories   44
strategic   88, 98, 130, 145, 164, 206, 233, 242
strategies   88, 97, 118, 128, 146, 153, 204, 221, 230-231
strategy   25, 37, 49, 56, 83, 86-87, 99, 108, 111, 114, 116,
141, 156, 190, 204, 217, 231, 250
stratify 192
Stream 64, 71
strengths   157, 257
stress   233
stretch 112
strict   65
strive   112
Strongly   13, 18, 30, 47, 62, 78, 95, 107
structural   239
structure   3-4, 79, 86, 111, 120, 154, 158-159, 161, 174, 220-
221, 233, 248
structured   119, 182

structures   141, 249
stubborn   112
stupid 108
subdivided   160
subject 10-11, 33
Subjective   192
subjects   63
submit 12
submitted   12, 228
subset 18
sub-teams   240
subtotals   184
succeed   54, 111
success   23, 28, 35-36, 40-41, 45, 48, 52, 56, 82, 84, 86, 88,
106, 109-110, 119, 121, 126, 157, 225, 230, 242, 246, 259-260, 265
successful   66, 87-88, 101, 109, 124, 130, 175, 185, 204, 224
succession   101
suddenly   209
sufficient   161, 245-246
suggest   233
suggested   106, 189
suitable   235, 254
summarize   176
summarized   161
summary   197, 249
supervisor   238
supplier   89, 112, 262
suppliers   45, 64, 116, 219, 261
supplies   262
supply 59
support   8, 25, 74, 80, 101, 104, 111, 118, 126, 135-136,
146, 173, 206, 231, 256
supported   69, 142, 211, 222
supporting   80, 103, 183, 194
supportive   199
surface   106
surprise 139
SUSTAIN   2, 90, 107
sustaining   102
symptom   18, 60
system 12-13, 32, 63, 103, 114, 116, 149-150, 156-157, 161, 164,
174, 196, 228, 231-233, 242, 246, 249, 251, 261-262
systematic   60, 162

systems   62, 67-68, 71, 76, 82, 99, 161, 190, 241, 252, 261
tables 190
tackle 60
tactics 139, 230-231
taking 47, 224, 237
talent 63
talents 107, 200
talking 8
target 34, 115, 140, 220-221
targeted   241
targets 112, 136, 251
tasked 97
technical   84, 134, 141, 150, 176, 226
technique   177
techniques   67, 114
technology   84, 169-170, 177, 208, 237, 254
templates   8, 10
tender 262
testable   34
test-cycle   194
tested 26
testing 87, 93, 149
Thamhain   176
thankful   9
themes240
themselves   116, 247
theories   176
theory 101
therein 161
things 81, 124, 134-135, 153, 205, 209
thinking   66, 92, 119
third-   86
thorough   92, 227
threat 20, 121
threaten   139
threats 145
through   68, 70, 116, 161, 242
throughout   1, 76, 128, 176, 232, 250, 267
tighter 107
time-bound   37
timeframe   64, 168, 186
timeframes   23
timeline   156, 192, 228

timely 22, 43, 89, 134, 204, 208, 214, 226, 238, 249, 268
timetable   171
Timing 236
together   196
toilet   233
tolerances   83
tolerated   165
tomorrow   97, 113
top-down   103
topics 84
toward 100, 224
towards   67, 141, 145
traceable   164
tracked   164, 177, 211
tracking   38, 98, 148
traction   108
trademark   1
trademarks   1
trade-offs   215
trained 32, 190-191, 208, 219
training   20, 22, 26-27, 72, 75, 87, 96, 99, 105, 143, 190,
220-221, 224, 233, 238, 242, 261, 268
trainings   21
Transfer   14, 29, 45, 61, 77, 94, 97, 99, 106, 132, 255
transition   115
translated   38
travel   238
trends 68-70, 93, 127, 140, 144, 212
trigger 83, 90
triggers 86
triple   218
trophy 113
trouble 128
trying   8, 110, 121, 147, 213
turnaround   168
ubiquitous   121
ultimate   126
unclear   32
underlying   79
undermine   121
understand   33, 70, 134, 198, 211, 238-240
understood   89, 117, 209
undertake   65

underway   80
uninformed   115
unique 122, 188
Unless 8
unresolved   173, 182
update   189, 265
updated   10-11, 72, 146, 171, 261
updates   11, 99, 255-256
upfront 220
upload 237
up-sell 120
urgency   208
usability   91, 130
useful 89, 101, 159, 205, 267
usefully 13, 18
UserID 169
utility   178
utilized 176, 241
utilizing 92
validate   60, 251
validated   30, 39, 44, 65, 76
Validation   242, 251
valuable   8
values 116, 161, 212
variables   71, 100, 231
Variance   6, 196, 249
-variance   183
variances   160-161, 176, 249-250
variation   18, 36, 64, 68, 100
variety 84
vendor 87, 134, 146, 182
vendors   25, 86, 163, 219
verbally   196
verified 11, 30, 39, 44, 65, 169
verify   47, 49, 53-60, 100, 105, 142, 241, 251, 263
verifying   48, 50-51, 53
version 256, 269
versions   35, 42
vertically   164
vested 118, 213
vetting 156
viable 98
viewpoint   265

viewpoints   265
vis-à-vis   208
vision   116, 144
visions 142
visits   146
visualize   178
voices 138
volatile 88
warrant   235
warranty   1
weaknesses   139, 157, 257
weather   139
weight 217
whether   8, 96, 109, 199
-which 208, 210
widespread   97
Wilemon   176
willing 188, 204
window   168
within   65, 82, 154, 163, 166, 178, 212, 221, 224, 228, 247, 258, 262
without1, 14, 119, 163, 208, 228, 240, 261, 263
worked   184, 210, 259
workers   108
workflow   66, 230
workforce   23, 93, 116, 129, 200
working   96, 102, 141, 181, 199, 207, 230, 267
work-life   198
Worksheet   4, 178, 186
worksheets   216
workshops   233
worst-case   35
writing 12, 151, 196
written 1, 254, 261
youhave   161
yourself   110, 125, 131, 199, 222

CPSIA information can be obtained
at www.ICGtesting.com
Printed in the USA
BVHW071107180719
553828BV00014B/1366/P